Through Darkest Gaul
with Trencher & Tastevin

John Whiting

Illustrations by Martin Sandhill
Foreword by Charles Shere

 Diatribal Press
London
1997

©1997 John Whiting, who has reluctantly acknowledged his moral responsibility as the author of this book. He is especially grateful to Anthony Rudolf for advice and assistance which made its publication possible, to Philip Keymer for round-the-clock technical wizardry, and to Mary for her constant help and encouragement.

Design, setting & camera-ready copy by Diatribal Press

Art work by
Martin Sandhill, Art & Design Services.
☎ +44 (0)181 442 1806 **F** + 44 (0)181 442 1053.

Representation and distribution in UK:
Central Books (Troika)
99 Wallis Road
Hackney Wick
London E9 5LN G.B.
☎ +44 (0)181 986 4854

Global distribution apart from North America:
Central Books

Distribution in North America:
SPD Inc.
1341 7th Street
Berkeley CA 94710-1403 USA
☎ +1 (510) 524 1668 **F** +1 (510) 524 0852 ⌨ spd@igc.apc.org

Published by
Diatribal Press
12 Hutchings Walk
Hampstead Garden Suburb
London NW11 6LT, G.B.
☎/ **F** +44 (0)181 458 1238 ⌨ diatribal@compuserve.com

ISBN 1-902110-00-5

∞ 10 9 8 7 6 5 4 3 2 1

First Edition

Printed at Alden Press
Oxford and Northampton

For Frank

_____

sine qua non

and

For Mary

_____

ne plus ultra

Contents

Preamble

Even before publication, this text had ambled further afield than its author. Half a hundred far-flung friends allowed me to e-mail it to them day by day, perhaps finding in it relief from the flood of messages advising them that the world was in terminal decline and that only their personal intervention with its leaders (Internet addresses helpfully appended) would save it from Armageddon. Some printed the installments out for their partners, who followed them religiously as a soup opera; others traced our progress over the *cols* and through the *gorges* on their Michelin road maps. For a few Caesars and Hannibals even more venerable than ourselves, it was an echo of bygone campaigns.

On one point there was consensus: I should see it into "hard copy". And so here we confront each other—you, who were intrigued, perhaps, by the cover; and I, who am trying to cajole you into buying it. My case is simple. I suggest that, if you are persuaded to make such a journey yourself, it will give you a great deal of pleasure. If, on the other hand, you decide that you need never visit these places, this book will have saved you a lot of money. Either way, you're ahead.

John Whiting
London
1997

Foreword
by Charles Shere

The art form of our time, the final thirty years of the twentieth century, has been the preparation of food. What the sonnet was to Elizabeth's London, the *Lied* to Schubert's Vienna, the easel painting to Impressionist Pontoise, the movie to the Nineteen-Thirties; that, to many of us, is the meal.

The art has always existed, of course, but it required a large general audience in order to become a major form, and that is what is new in our time. Easier world travel, greater disposable income, dissatisfaction with the unimaginative and mass-market-dominated cuisine of the pre-1968 epoch, new entertainment-industry stars like Julia Child and Martha Stewart, and God's own quantity of popular books, magazines, and television shows: all these have given cuisine a place once occupied by religion, football, whist, or the waltz.

What's been missing is the voice for traditional values, a little bit of reassuring constancy in the face of trend. This book provides such a voice, querulous at times, given to bad puns and an occasional elbow in the rib, but aware of that ineffable quality, Quality.

I suppose I have myself to blame for this book, at least in part. Over the years I've kept journals while traveling, and one or two have been set in type and distributed among a small circle of friends, no more than a dozen, as annoying little demonstrations of my industry and superciliousness. One, describing three weeks in Paris in 1977, caught John's eye. Recognizing me as a fine *bouche*, he asked for recommendations. Not suspecting he would make them stock in trade, I acquiesced.

Then, in the summer of 1996, I traveled with a laptop, sending e-mail reports of the trip to a few friends. Since a visit to John in London was about to terminate my European holiday, it seemed appropriate to let him know what recent adventures would have prepared me for the delights of St. James's tables.

The laptop will soon have revolutionized amateur journalism, the daily writing-up of daily adventures, whether for later reflection or for the immediate sharing with friends. E-mail has of course greatly facilitated the latter process, as John demonstrated a couple of pages back. The epistolary nonfiction narrative is the literary form for our day. This born-again medium, the quasi-public journal, finds in John a perfect tool. He is a writer, by which I mean he inexorably writes. He is a machine that ingests food and drink and spins out words.

I don't want you to think John lives only for the table. Along the way he admires scenery, curses road-signs, acknowledges architecture, glances at works of art. If he has little patience for a certain type of contemporary art, who can blame him? He knows a sculptural Big Mac when it comes between him and his *bouillabaisse*.

He admires industry and dedication in others, and regrets their decrease. He knows that few human endeavors are as chaotic as restaurants. He suspects, I think, that the great restaurants involve highly gifted artists, particularly excellent provender, and enough diners to keep the creditors at bay. Such restaurants are squeezed among contending forces: the weather, unpredictable interruptions of market supply, follies and the madness of crowds, the stock market, and God knows what other influences.

There must be enough demand to keep the industry going, but not so much as to exhaust its raw materials or to overcome the dedication of the *restaurateur*. This latter must be a dedicated maniac willing to work eighteen hours a day in the heat and limelight of a highly publicized kitchen for the pleasure of hearing the complaints of the customers, each of whom believes he knows more of the theory and history of any dish than does the chef.

As John concludes, insatiable curiosity will survive all this. I was drawn to l'Auberge de l'Atre Fleuri by a marvelous book, Roy Andries de Groot's *The Auberge of the Flowering Hearth*. When I got there in 1974 it was changed; the elderly ladies who ran it had sold it; the new owners were gifted but had to deal with travelers whose expectations had been unrealistically inflated by de Groot's nostalgia and fantasy. (He was blind, poor man, and forced to rely on others' eyes, not always reliable in their eagerness to please.) The old Auberge, and the bucolic setting of la Grande Chartreuse, are not what they were a quarter century ago; perhaps they never were.

John is philosophical in the face of the present, though occasionally raging at the threat of the future. He is patient with his own impatience, which is a mark of generosity. He is eager to learn, and to listen. He is a good traveling companion, particularly now that we can simply shove him into the glove box and continue on our way, hauling him out to consult at the odd moment when D520 unaccountably fails to lead us to that village shrine to gastronomy we dimly recall his celebrating.

Give John a ride on your next trip. He asks little.

Berkeley, California, August 1997

Mary Whiting

Part 1: Two Old Codgers in a Jalopy

One needs only to be old enough in order to be as young as one will.
Henry Adams, *Mont-Saint-Michel and Chartres*

London Monday October 7, 1996

The Lonesome Traveler now has company: a virtual secretary that sits in his lap and takes down everything he says. From tomorrow, it will faithfully transcribe a three weeks' slow drive around the periphery of France, with no fixed commitment except a concert in Rouen, two weeks hence. I've died and gone to heaven!

I'll have human companionship as well. Frank is an old UC Berkeley friend going back to the 1950s. Over the decades we've met up in London, Paris, Darmstadt, Chicago or wherever for sight-seeing, concert-going and conversation. For years Frank has been urging me to find time for a tour of France.

—The University of Chicago ran a terrific Impressionist package tour to Nice and the southeast (he's told me more than once) but it was expensive. I've still got the itinerary. Maybe we could work it in.

This year it's finally happening. Frank can't drive the van, but he'll be able to navigate, a service I could really use in French cities. The villages are no problem. Unlike America, the smaller the town, the clearer the road signs—every alternative is marked. But in the cities the highway numbers are usually missing and the roads are indicated only with their destinations, which often change from one intersection to the next. When the local route numbers do appear, they bear no relationship to what you find in the Michelin Atlas. Apparently chosen by a committee of numerologists and astrologers, they seem to alter with the phases of the moon.

Early tomorrow morning Frank and I drive to Folkstone to take the catamaran to Boulogne, less than an hour's flight. It's "flights" on cats and hovercraft rather than sailings, which allows them to rope off a few seats, call them "Club Class", and then rip off passengers for occupying them. These fortunate few are also allowed to drive on board early, thus saving perhaps a couple of minutes at the other end. The real bonus, of course, is an invisible badge which reads, I AM BETTER THAN YOU.

The plan is to drive down the east side of France to Nice; then across the bottom, with an upward diversion in the middle to the Massif Central and the Gorges du Tarn, then back down into Gascony and up the west side by way of the Île de Ré and Golfe du Morbihan and thence through Brittany and Normandy back to Boulogne. Traced on a map, our projected route looks a bit like the rear view of a crouching small-headed Matisse nude. After two weeks we'll make a mad dash to Rouen from wherever we are for the concert, and then a return dash two days later to resume our *mois de pèlerinage*.

The game plan is to keep it cheap: we'll sleep in the van (where I've laid out a couple of beds), breakfast on muesli and cafetière coffee prepared over our little Gaz cooker, lunch on picnics garnered from *boulangerie* and *fromagerie* along the way, and then settle down in the evening for a serious dinner at a picturesque *auberge* specializing in the local cuisine. But Frank has been warned that our first meal away from London will also be the most expensive. The first night's destination will inevitably be Longuyon and Monsieur Tisserant—the *menu degustation* at Le Mas and a hotel room to sleep it off. Hang the expense! It's one of the best unsung restaurants in France.

With an early start, we should be able to follow my usual N43 route from Calais towards Metz and Strasbourg, with a side trip into the Ardennes Forest in Belgium along the Semois. The latter is, in Michelin-ese, worth a detour. As you approach Frahan the N819 suddenly comes out at the edge of a cliff overlooking a vast horseshoe bend in the river, a sight to send the easily distracted driver straight into an oncoming truck. It would be a suitable subject for one of those late mediaeval Belgian landscapes which seem to be afraid they might leave something out. Then back down to the N43 at Montmedy to storm its fortress, and thence the few remaining kilometers to Longuyon and gastronomic bliss.

The second day should take us down the motorway from Longwy to Nancy and then across the Vosges to Hunnawihr, staying overnight at the Sip-Mack cellars. Then a longer drive to the Massif de Chartreuse, with a stop at Colmar to pay our profound respects to the Isenheim altarpiece by

Matthias Grünewald. And finally, skirting the Alpes-Maritimes to Nice, arriving on Friday evening so as to meet Robin, a friend of Frank's, for lunch on Saturday. Together with lots of sightseeing, it'll be four days' hard driving; but what rewards!

When I e-mailed London food writer Richard Ehrlich about our plans, he kindly sent me his review copy of Mirabel Osler's *A Spoon with Every Course: In Search of the Legendary Food of France*. Although she writes in detail about almost two dozen restaurants, it is not so much a guide book as an extended essay on what is happening to French eating habits: an indispensable source of information on the past, the present, and the ominous future. From my own experience, one can no longer just drop in at a provincial restaurant and expect to find simple wholesome examples of traditional local cuisine. But it still exists: our mission is to boldly go in search of it.

Longuyon Tuesday October 8

Our first stop along the N43 to Longuyon is at Le Cateau-Cambrésis for a dive straight into modern art history. It's the birthplace of Matisse; the Palais Fénelon, once the residence of the Bishops of Cambrais, contains a museum devoted to his work. Arriving just after noon we find the gates shut. A quick perusal of the sign reveals that the palace is closed for lunch between twelve and two. Should we wait?

I've already seen it but it's worth visiting again, particularly as Frank is very fond of Matisse and is unlikely to return. We kill a couple of hours walking slowly along the main street. It's a dusty, not particularly arresting wide place in the road, but it's French and it's the first town we've stopped in. Even so, two hours is a long time to stay interested in small shops displaying nondescript merchandise. Being non-French-speakers (i.e., uncouth barbarians), even the leisurely perusal of a newspaper is beyond us.

Two o'clock arrives and we stroll back to the museum, to find the gates still firmly shut. Further examination reveals a small notice at the bottom of the sign, *Fermé Lundi et Mardi*. Our French pocket dictionary tells us that this means we still have a twenty-four hour wait. When does the time spent in learning rudimentary French arrive at break-even point?

A couple of hours later when we divert into Belgium the 5 a.m. departure has taken its toll on Frank, who starts to nod off in spite of the twisting roads; but he awakens to find the panorama above the Samois in the Ardennes as impressive as I had promised. By the time we arrive in the late afternoon the sun has lent the landscape a roseate flush and the great horseshoe bend of the river is highlighted with touches of gold. The trees with their brilliant fall colors look as though they might have been transplanted from Vermont in a vintage year. There's a hotel just behind us: what must it be like to live through the changing seasons with such a view! A garbage can rattles as a kitchen helper empties a bucket of scraps. He goes back inside without even glancing up.

Once we are out of the mountains onto the N43 again, the sky is as blue as Provence on a clear summer's day. There, framed against it, is Montmedy, the ramparts of its 16th century citadel high above the town enclosing the massive twin-towered church of St. Martin. I've passed it many times, the road winding up to the brow of the hill, where the ground suddenly levels off on all sides like the magic kingdom at the top of the beanstalk. Such a luminous late afternoon. Finally I can stop to look.

A narrow road winds around the high walls, crosses a portcullis and passes between stone towers which must have been specially designed to only just admit our VW Transporter. Around a sharp bend, through another pair of gates, and we're in a large open square surrounded with several centuries of stonework in various stages of restoration. In an upper story of one derelict building is a hand-lettered sign reading, *Droit de restauration, droit de vivre.* Two other neglected buildings bear similar cryptic messages. Is the restoration of the citadel curtailed from lack of funds? Is it being carried out contrary to the wishes of the community? I step into the only open business on the square, identifiable by the photocopier visible through the window.

The young lady in charge speaks excellent English and is happy to explain the mystery. The three derelict buildings belong to a single owner, an irascible fellow whose nose was put out of joint when someone was allowed to open a café across the street next to the museum, in competition with his own dreary establishment. In a fury, he closed up shop, posted his protests, and went away. He refuses to sell and the buildings quietly rot. The *restauration* of both architecture and anatomy is thus aborted. In the end, it turns out to be just a case of *droit de seigneur*.

Those who know me are aware that the primary purpose of my trips through France is to consume a *menu degustation* at Le Mas in Longuyon, a dying town in Lorraine on the edge of Luxembourg. This will be the third within a month, and they are never the same. Unlike some cautious celebrity chefs, M. Tisserant offers, not an unvarying selection of conventional luxury courses such as *foie gras*, truffles and lobster, but an improvised seven-course sampling menu based on what the market offered that morning. Mary and I once ordered it on two successive days, both without advance warning, and were served dinners as different but as distinctive as two sets of Mozart variations.

Le Mas still has a Michelin *macaron*, but the expense of maintaining such a reputation is more than most restaurants in the region can now support. Gérard Tisserant, who inherited the Hotel Lorraine to which Le Mas is attached, was able to build its clientele through the trade which came from the iron industry. And then the bottom fell out of coal, steel, and the whole complex which was the region's livelihood. M. Tisserant found himself saddled with a fine restaurant which few could be bothered to find and nobody would buy from him. The result was that a man who had held the honorific title of *premier sommelier* for all of France had to pull in his horns and rely on those who were prepared to make the journey to a far corner of the country just to honor his cuisine. He has told the mayor that the town should be paying taxes to him rather than he to the town, because tourists only come there to eat at his restaurant.

And indeed they do. During the off season he brings in customers and staves off boredom by scheduling weekends in which music and food complement each other. A fixed *menu degustation* is offered on an occasional Friday and Saturday night, each accompanied by live music which may be classical, folk or cabaret. Guests may opt for one or both nights, with or without hotel accommodation. The most expensive weekend package is around 1200 francs—in Paris, the price of a solitary lunch with a modest bottle *chez* Joel Robuchon. M. Tisserant sends out mailings to interested persons.

The most memorable meal I ate there was in 1991 when one of my stopovers coincided with a Saturday night dinner with *musique de table* provided by a wind ensemble of professors from the conservatory at Nancy. Between courses we were treated to stunningly idiomatic performances of Poulenc, Milhaud, Satie et al, interspersed with idiosyncratic but exciting interpretations of Mozart and Beethoven. Everyone stopped talking and listened. I felt that I was a privileged participant in a total event, in which concert and cuisine flowed seamlessly into one another. I was so inspired that after dinner I called Eric Mottram in London to share it with him. Thenceforth I was the Epicurean who had phoned from France in the middle of the night to anatomize a meal.

Frank's habitual self-indulgences lie in the food-for-thought categories of opera, plays and concerts, and so the price of the *menu degustation* at 400 francs brings a sudden hiatus in his conversation, like Jack Benny when the robber demanded his money or his life: . . .*I'm thinking! I'm thinking!* But he decides to go with the flow. Today it includes four *écrevisses*—two each—brought live to the table before being cooked in a light wine sauce so as not to mask their delicate flavor. These, I tell Frank authoritatively, have been brought by train from Boulogne to the station just across the road. Every guide book that mentions Le Mas offers this explanation for the freshness of its produce.

The next morning after breakfast M. Tisserant asks if we had enjoyed our meal.

—Superb as usual, especially the crayfish.

—I'm glad you liked them. They're hard to get now in France. These were flown in from Australia.

—Flown in from Australia? I thought all your seafood was delivered by train!

—Alas, no more. SNCF can no longer be bothered with local food deliveries, so everything must come by truck. There used to be fish and vegetable stalls at every station along the route, but now they are all closed.

—But where do the local people shop?

A Gallic shrug.

—Almost everyone goes to the supermarkets. I still have my own sources but I can't get exactly what I want every day.

—At least you've had a fairly busy night for a Tuesday.

—Yes, thanks to the Belgians and the Luxembourgers and the Germans. They're my best customers during the winter. Some drive for an hour or more to get here and then stay overnight, so they can drink as much as they like without having to breathe into a little bag. This is a poor region; if I were to charge only what the local people can afford I would have to use inferior ingredients and I would lose my reputation. And then, Monsieur, you would not come here any more!

M. Tisserant goes on to tell me that the restaurants with Michelin *macarons* (i.e., stars, as they are commonly called in English) have dropped by a quarter in the last ten years because the clientele has steadily diminished. I've read that French bistros and auberges, the places the locals always went to, are going bust at the rate of 2000 per year! And every small town in France now has a sign by the road as you enter, telling you where to find the *double arches d'or*. Two factors are responsible: a new generation of consumers who are unwilling to sit for two or three hours savoring their food, and new trainees who refuse to face the lifelong prospect of being out at the market at five in the morning, in the kitchen cooking all day, then supervising the clean-up and, if they are friendly with the staff, unwinding over drinks until after midnight. Nevertheless, there are still young fanatics who are eager to try. But if you are a restaurant owner, why pay someone to spend all day assembling what you can buy for half the price in little frozen packets? Fire the chef and hire a press agent.

Even the great chefs of Paris, who you'd expect to be fireproof, have opened little bistros next door to attract the un-rich. But they have found that, instead of making more money, they're merely losing less. Except for a fortunate few, the gourmet restaurant business is becoming like the old Woody Allen gag:

– I've got a new job: I'm the dresser at a burlesque house.
– Wow! What's the pay?
– A hundred a week.
– That's not very much.
– Yeah, I know, but it's all I can afford.

Hotel de Lorraine, Restaurant Le Mas, rue de la Gare,
   54260 Longuyon ☎ 03 82 26 50 85 **F** 03 82 39 26 09

Hunawihr Wednesday October 9

The journey from northern Lorraine to southern Alsace—two parts of France which are commonly lumped together—contains within its short compass such contrasts as to suggest the rich variety of scenery and cuisine within this single country. I could spend a lifetime of days and dinners exploring what this stubbornly individualistic country has to offer. Charles de Gaulle once remarked that it was impossible to govern a country with 350 cheeses. I would happily devote my life to sampling them, particularly now that they are all under threat from American food vandals who are seriously campaigning to outlaw unpasteurized cheeses throughout the world. We Americans, alas, tend to fall into two categories: those with taste but no power and those with power but no taste. In the face of such a juggernaut, even France's legendary intransigence, long the savior of its ethnic and gastronomic identity by means of an unashamedly reactionary agricultural policy, is finally proving insufficient to insulate its unique, delicately-balanced food network from the seismic encroachment of the chip mountain and the megaburger.

If you approach Alsace, not from the north by way of Strasbourg, but from the west across the Vosges mountains, the contrast is all the more dramatic. Geographically, it is more naturally allied to Germany than to France, with only the Rhine to separate them. This shows in the architecture, the folk art, and especially in the food and wine, which are Germanic in their names and ingredients but with a French delicacy and sophistication.

So far I've not needed the services of a navigator. These are roads I've traveled so often that I hardly need to glance at a map. There are other routes I might have followed to south-east France along inviting unfamiliar byways, but one of the joys of traveling with a companion, particularly if it's someone you've been close to for a long time, is to be Virgil to his Dante, relishing the sighs of pleasure and the gasps of astonishment as you turn the pages of your private picture book.

A free motorway gets you from Longwy to Nancy, and the N59 thence to St Die, from where you can elect either the old Ste-Marie tunnel or the N415 which takes you over the top. Either way you arrive at the Alsatian Wine Route between Molsheim and Guebwiller—the names tell you that you're well within the German sphere of influence.

Since our object is sightseeing rather than celerity, I've chosen to come even further south towards Gerardmer and then up the mountains almost to the top to join the Route des Crêtes, a roller coaster ride of hairpin bends and sheer cliffs which was carved into the west side of the Vosges during World War I in order to conceal French troop movements from the Germans. (If reconnaissance planes had been invented just a little earlier, it would never have been built and we'd now have to hike it.) The guide books tell you to be prepared for breath-taking thrills, but these are more plentiful on the way up. As soon as you get onto the Route des Crêtes itself you are aware that it has been sanitized. The road is now wide enough to allow tour buses to pass each other, and the sheer drops are well guarded by railings and stone walls. In mid-October we're between tourist seasons, but new invaders are about to overrun the hills. Unwilling to wait for the first snow, troops of earnest apprentices wearing cumbersome roller-bottomed training skis have turned the road into an asphalt nursery slope. The sheer acreage of parking lots, though empty, gives eloquent warning of what is to come. If you want peace and quiet, stay away when the hiking and skiing seasons are at their peak.

As you come down towards the wine country the road becomes almost suburban, with frequent up-market housing estates, well-tended curbs and neat uniform signs. Then you enter the productive vineyard area of *Appellation Controlée* vineyards and the calendar is turned back. This land is too valuable to waste on domestic real estate.

The Alsatians could have taught Walt Disney Inc. a thing or two. Long before Hollywood was giving us chintz and lederhosen, Alsace had perfected the theme park. All along the Wine Route from Strasbourg to Colmar are villages full of Snow White cottages with rustic roofs, carved cornices and pastel plaster, where busloads of glassy-eyed tourists stagger from winery to winery until they can't tell a Gewurztraminer from a Weimaraner. At the end of a bleary afternoon they're back in their hotels with a headache and a horn-handled corkscrew.

Riquewihr, "one of France's most visited towns", is the apotheosis of the picturesque. Cleared of coaches and sightseers it would be charming, but this never occurs. The Blue Guide says, with massive understatement, "unfortunately the place can get uncomfortably crowded during weekends and in the summer." Crowded? It makes Venice feel like a ghost town.

Ribeauville is where the serious buying and selling takes place. A couple of kilometers north of it is Hunawihr, just a signpost along the way for the guide books but in fact a miniature Riquewihr of lived-in and worked-in houses of equal charm and distinction. The huge *négociants*, such as Hugel, are located where the crowds congregate, but Hunawihr has its own respected names, including Sipp-Mack, the producer of a fine Gewurztraminer V.T., a distinguished Rosacker Grand Cru Riesling, and a *Crémant*, which is the term which replaced *méthode champenoise* when the latter was outlawed in the EEC, the word champagne being too holy to be applied to any bottle not requiring a second mortgage. Sipp-Mack also bottle an Edelzwicker, a mixed-grape *ordinaire* which, at 26 francs a litre, must be one of the cheapest really good light quaffing wines going.

With commissions from a couple of friends, I've some moderately serious tasting to do. It's time to use the spittoon. I'm a Quaff-Mack rather than a Sipp-Mack, so it's a device I generally eschew, but I once had a close call with a breathalizing *gendarme* in the Loire and I don't want to push my luck. I assume that the young man tending the shop speaks German, so we stagger along for a few minutes until he asks politely, in an American accent, if we might speak English. He turns out to be a member of the family, with an American wife, and widely traveled; it takes no time at all to establish that he loves the San Francisco area, has been to Kermit Lynch's wine shop in Berkeley, and has read his wonderful book, *Adventures on the Wine Route*, in English. (An indication of its authenticity is that it has been selling well in a French translation.) He also visited Chez Panisse but couldn't make time to eat there. His wife is both a *sommelier* and a pastry chef, and at the mention of Lindsey Shere, pastry chef at Chez Panisse since its beginning, his voice takes on a reverential tone. There are True Believers, even in the foothills of the Vosges.

The negative side of Sipp-Mack's superb location is that, because it is a little way up the hillside at the back of a village which is itself off the beaten track, the tour buses don't stop at its door. In order to introduce more people to the wines, the family built a bed-and-breakfast annex, which is how I discovered them. Listed in the first edition of Alastair Sawday's *Guide to French Bed and Breakfast*, it turned out to be slightly hostel-like but very clean, cheap and comfortable and a perfect location from which to explore both the village and the whole Alsatian wine route. The first time I stayed there I met a German who had been coming back for years and whose map of Alsace was a spider's web of marked routes which he regularly visited. A man who could obviously afford to stay wherever he wished, he chose to base himself at Sipp-Mack in Hunnawihr. —It is real, he said, obviating all further discussion.

This is where we'd planned to stay tonight, but this time the season works against us. It's the middle of the grape harvest and no hands can be spared to service the rooms. Now, if we were prepared to stop and pick grapes. . . .

We're sent down the hill to a non-vintner neighbor who might be able to accommodate us. There we strike it lucky—a huge bed-sitting room with ancient wooden beams and stone fireplace, formerly an indoor grape-treading space, which Madame Seiler lets us have for a knock-down off-season 280 francs. Just across the street is the Relais du Poète, where I've previously enjoyed a good simple *choucroute*. We're set up for the night, with plenty of time for a side trip to Riquewihr, the Alsatian Disneyland. It's a struggle-pit I usually avoid, but Frank should see it as a part of his education.

Once again October proves to be the ideal touring season. This being midweek we are able to find a parking space just outside the walls—though not without a search—and walk back to the main Gothic-arched gate where the foot-sore pilgrims are allowed to enter. Even at this time of year the gentle upward slope of the main street is crowded, though not elbow-jostling. Along it's entire length every building is devoted at the ground floor to the emptying of wallets. You can buy pallets of cheap glass and crockery, giant hogsheads of hogswill, yards of pseudo-peasant machine embroidery, and acres of jolly postcards showing your friends why you are too drunk to write to them. One shop owner, perhaps a rejected applicant for a symphony orchestra desk, poses in front of his shop in lederhosen, competently performing a wide-ranging repertoire on his clarinet, with taped Music-Minus-One accompaniment. The profound boredom with which he answers our questions suggests that he would rather be elsewhere.

Well disguised and requiring careful attention to identify them are a few shops selling serious merchandise: delicatessens with excellent sausages and cheeses; the principle sales rooms of Hugel, one of the most distinguished and reliable *négociants* of Alsacian wine; and the best beer shop I've encountered anywhere in the world, well-stocked with the products of American boutique breweries, a large assortment of Belgian Trappistes, and the fabled strong dark beer from Weihenstephan, the centuries-old state brewery of Bavaria. The latter I've only encountered in the now sadly defunct *Herrenmühle*, a mad Munich chef's labor of love which used to draw me like a siren's song into the Taunus north of Frankfurt.

Tired of the high-pressure jostle, Frank and I head down a side-street and prove yet again that the main street of any tourist node is a black hole of imploding energy which draws everything into itself. If you can resist the centripetal force and fight your way outward past its periphery, you'll discover the tranquillity of isolation. We wander the quiet residential streets observed only by a few curious natives who are not accustomed to seeing strangers more than a few feet away from the epicenter.

Back in Hunawihr we settle down for an hour's conversation over a litre of Sipp-Mack Edelzwicker and then stroll across the street for a simple meal at the Relais du Poète. Inside we find a bustling up-market restaurant with crisp white linen, elegant china and crystal, and multi-lingual menus offering multi-cultural fare. In spite of its Cinderella-like transformation the prices are still reasonable, so we settle down defiantly in our shabby sweaters. This being the game season, I go straight to the venison and am served a hearty stew which would not disappoint in a peasant's cottage. I remind myself not to be prejudiced either way by a restaurant's ambiance.

After dinner, an affable conversation with the new owner-chef, who speaks serviceable English, reveals that he is Swiss and that he relies in the off-season on a steady stream of Germans to keep him busy. A pattern has thus been set within two nights which threatens to repeat itself. Our search for the legendary kitchens of rural France threatens to become a quest for the Holy Grail.

Le Relais de Poète, Patrice et Catherine Wespy, 6 rue du Nord,
    68150 Hunawihr
François Sipp-Mack, 1 rue des Vosges, 68150 Hunawihr,
    Haut-Rhin ☎ 03 89 73 61 88

St-Pierre-de-Chartreuse Thursday October 10

My peaceful slumber after a good meal was interrupted early this morning by "noises off". Opening one eye, I could see Frank at the table in the middle of the room under a hanging lamp, rifling through a stack of papers. A look at my watch told me it was three-thirty. Three-thirty in the morning! I'm not prepared for this. The van was sitting just outside in an enclosed courtyard, its beds ready for occupancy. Muttering something politely incoherent, I put on my dressing gown and stumbled outdoors. Inside the van it was very cold but very quiet. As the sleeping bag warmed up, I tried to imagine the adjacent one occupied by an inveterate snorer as loud and constant as myself, our stentorian battle cries reverberating around the metal shell. Impossible. Our earplugs would be as useless as parasols in a monsoon. It will have to be hotels all the way. After all, it's only money.

Later it's time for embarrassing admissions: Frank misread his watch, thinking it was five-thirty, and my own high-tech international Cassio had reverted to English Summer Time. The truth—four-thirty a.m.—lay midway between us. But an expensive lesson has been learned: neither of us will get any sleep stuffed like two grampuses into a big tin can.

With the possible exception of the mad dash to Rouen in a couple of weeks, this has probably been the longest day's drive of the trip, partly by design and partly by accident. We'd reached the stage of the journey when I needed some expert navigation. The plan today was to visit the Unterlinden Museum in Colmar in the morning, then drive south through Switzerland in order to save time on the excellent Swiss mountain highways coming out at Geneva and thence by way of the A40 and A41 to Chambery. There we'd take the N6 down the western edge of the Massif de la Chartreuse to St-Laurent-du-Pont, where we'd cut east through and over the mountains to St-Pierre-de-Chartreuse.

Since we're trying to make good time to Nice, why this long side-trek into the middle of nowhere? Because of my solid faith in the taste of Charles Shere, with whom a long friendship spans the worlds of music, non-commercial radio, and gastronomy. When I asked him a couple of years ago which French provincial hotel/restaurants he particularly remembered, he harked back some twenty years to a simple *auberge* beside a mountain stream. The chances of it remaining unchanged were virtually nil, but I had already traveled through this divinely unspoiled country at Charles' recommendation and was certain that, even if his small hotel had been taken over by Holiday Inn, there would be another nearby that wouldn't disappoint; I had seen several such places last time through.

Colmar would be worth half-a-day's delay in setting out because it contains one of the most richly reverberant works of art in Western Europe. The Isenheim altarpiece by Matthias Grünewald is a masterpiece which has multi-layered associations not only with his own politically blighted career, but also with Hindemith's Sisyphean composition of his great biographical opera *Matthis der Mahler*. With no hope of a performance, Hindemith nevertheless devoted himself to telling the painter's story in such a way as to prefigure his own, aborted by Hitler's rise to power.

Almost fifty years ago, before I even knew the name of Grünewald, I took a modern music course at College of the Pacific which was taught by a young Hindemith enthusiast who spent the first month taking us through the *Matthis der Mahler* suite: three densely constructed movements based on the inner panels of the Isenheim altarpiece. No reproductions of it were used in the lecture/demonstrations—looking back to those pre-multi-media days, this may have been deliberate—but by the end I felt as though I could listen to the Hindemith suite and see the three primary panels entire. Forty years later, when I stood long before them in Colmar, the Hindemith played itself through in my inner ear. Messiaen's assertion that music showed him colors didn't seem so strange.

We arrive as planned at opening time, but busloads of eager tourists are there before us. By the time we've found the triptych, a solid phalanx of Japanese art-lovers bars the way. The wings of the altarpiece are detached and exhibited together behind the center panel, so that there are four positions from which a part of it can be viewed from either the front or the rear: both sides of every panel are painted. The next few minutes are spent dodging back and forth from panel to panel, avoiding the complex military maneuvers with which the tour guide takes them through its interrelated geography. At least, being in an unfamiliar language, the lecture holds only the distraction of noise, not of invasive thought.

After a while Frank wanders off. Catching up with him, I apologize for the distraction as if I've been somehow responsible.

—That's OK, he says, I'm really more interested in modern art. Wasn't there a poster outside about a visiting Otto Dix show? Let's go find it.

The next hour is spent in close examination of this later German's exploration of man's inhumanity to man: interesting in its own right, but not exactly in a class with Grünewald. *De gustibus. . . .*

The exit door from the museum brings us out onto a square opposite a new Monoprix supermarket. The time and the opportunity coincide to get some bread, cheese and paté for lunch. In the center of a prosperous town, this is the new breed of Monoprix. It's an urban shopping mall: hundreds of luxury items including maybe three dozen fine cheeses, rows of terrines in picturesque pottery dishes, exotic salads, pre-cooked meats, endless cases of frozen meals ready to pop in the microwave and tuck into while watching a celebrity chef on TV—in fact, a thousand good reasons for the busy homemaker just to buy everything needed for the week all together under one roof. Neighborhood shops? Useful in case of memory lapses or unexpected guests.

After lunch we still have most of the driving ahead of us. On the A35 down to Basel I remember my heart-in-mouth panic a couple of months before when the Swiss customs demanded a fortune in Swiss francs to take my sound equipment across the border for a couple of days. Today the equipment is minimal and packed under the false floor, with our suitcases piled in front of it. I can look them straight in the eye and say, truthfully, that we're just on our way through.

Customs officers, like dogs, can smell fear. This time they wave us cheerily on our way, not even glancing at our proffered passports.

Going through Switzerland is a last-minute inspiration, so I haven't brought a Swiss map. No problem. Once on the motorway, I only have to look for signs to Bern, then Lausanne, then Geneva. What could be simpler? I reckoned without a sudden brainstorm. Bern is indicated, then Bern plus Luzern. Luzern? Isn't that the German name for Lausanne? Never mind, they're in the same direction. Then a motorway junction indicates Bern one way, Luzern the other. Time for instant decision. No help from my navigator; no map for him to look at. Let's go for Luzern. After a while, signs to Aarau appear. That's to the north. Then signs to Basel. My God, that's back where we started! A stop at a motorway service area reveals that we've hooked north on the wrong motorway. So it's a U-turn and back towards Bern.

That little piece of stupidity has cost us an hour of daylight driving time. Only when we arrive at our hotel does Frank remember that he has a map of Europe, including Switzerland, in his bag of guide books. After bawling him out, I wipe a four-egg soufflé off my face when I discover that the layout of the Swiss motorways is clearly indicated on the route planning map at the front of my Michelin motoring atlas of France. Dunce caps all round.

We still arrive at Chambery in the late afternoon, with ample time to reach our hotel before nightfall. Just find the N6 and skirt the edge of the Massif de la Chartreuse, leaving its exploration until next day. Navigation is now essential. As we thread our way through the labyrinth of feeder roads, no route numbers are given; only an alphabet soup of unfamiliar destinations. Frank stares at the map in bewilderment as I call out painfully anglicized French place names—no time to work out proper pronunciations. At last the magic words MASSIF DE LA CHARTREUSE appear on a tiny sign and I swerve to make the turning. A narrow road climbs abruptly into foothills, rising ever more steeply. We've taken, not the N6, but the route which leads over the top of the Massif, a road which becomes a Grand Prix course of steep ascents and hairpin bends. It's too late to do anything except go for it.

The breath-taking vistas I've looked forward to showing Frank become fleeting side views along an obstacle course which must be negotiated within the hour. At least I'm back on familiar roads, but I've never been to the hotel and know only the name of the nearest village. In fact, I was unable to phone ahead and don't even know for certain that it's open, only that my two-year-old Michelin says it should be. A few hotels flash by, all of them closed. This may be the night we sleep in the van somewhere in the middle of nowhere, with only fierce wild animals and an armed, indignant land-owner for company.

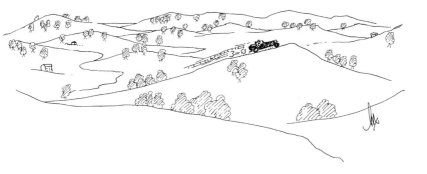

It's still light enough to see the scale of the mountains and I can appreciate that this early evening vista is different from what I've seen before in the clear light of midsummer. But poor Frank's eyes are glued to the road. Though not a religious man, he is mentally crossing himself.

Just outside St-Pierre-de-Chartreuse is a freshly-painted roadside sign announcing L'ATRE FLEURI. But the tiny main street of the village yields only one lit-up hotel that might be a fall-back. A villager tells us to continue a few kilometers south towards Grenoble and we'll find it on our left. Watching carefully for a building which might very well be unlit, we come around a bend and are met with cheery lights and the magic sign. I pull into the parking lot and dash inside. Yes, they are open. Yes, they have a vacant room with two beds. No, we are not too late for dinner. Jason seizing the Golden Fleece could not have been more ecstatic.

l'Atre Fleuri proves to be a rustic, unpretentious hotel in the midst of a forest, overlooking a bubbling mountain stream. It was taken over six months ago by a hopeful young couple, she officiating in the kitchen and he front-of-house, with a kitchen helper and a waitress to fill in as needed. The wife speaks comprehensible English. No, she assures me, they do not plan to change anything. I note sadly that the menu is now like everywhere else, a printed list of set dinners. Yes, it is what people expect. But she doesn't try to keep everything available all the time. Rather than stock a freezer, certain items are sometimes not available. What about tonight? The restaurant is almost empty. Does she have anything local and freshly produced?

We're in luck. It's Thursday and she has a crowd coming for the weekend, so she has been laying in generous supplies of fresh ingredients and has already cooked in advance certain things that will keep refrigerated and not have to be frozen. I start with a cheesy gratin of fresh salmon, then tasty marinated and stewed rabbit. On the wine list, to my delight, is a Bandol rosé, a wine which rarely travels far from home without being consumed somewhere along the way. And all for around 150 francs, including half the shared bottle of wine.

We've gambled and hit the jackpot. Up in our room we open the window and listen to the gurgling of the stream below. Nothing is more comforting at night than the sound of tumbling water—unless it is accompanied by the rumbling grunts of a snoring roommate. Regretfully we stuff in our ear plugs and the stream is silenced.

l'Atre Fleuri, Route du Col de Porte, 38380 St-Pierre-de-Chartreuse
☎ 04 76 88 60 21 **F** 04 76 88 64 97

Nice Friday October 11

This morning the early sun reveals that we have indeed been admitted to paradise. The mountains are not high, the scale is reassuringly human—and bovine, with cows munching contentedly in the neighboring pastures. Here too the fall colors are New-England brilliant. The illusion is complete when we turn around and see, at the far end of a straight road, a sign with a golden double arch, reassuring us that we will find a Big Mac and French fries waiting for us in Grenoble. What more could life hold?

In daylight, St-Pierre-de-Chartreuse proves to be the meeting point of several valleys, so that whichever way you look you are at the bottom of a mountain. An enthusiastic hiker could spend a week or more taking off every morning in a different direction. The countryside is so unspoiled that your car could also have a holiday, not needed even to reach the start of yet another achingly beautiful path. I can imagine returning every night from a vigorous hike (or in my case, a leisurely stroll) and sitting down at a table overlooking the stream for a simple, hearty meal. Demi-pension is less than 250 francs per day. But don't tell too many people, only just enough to keep this paradise solvent.

Having traversed the Massif de la Chartreuse, though at breakneck pace, it hardly seems worth going back, and the famous monastery which used to produce the pure, elegant green and yellow liqueurs isn't open to the public, so we drive westerly along the Gorge du Grier Mort to St-Laurent, which should have been the last leg of our route the night before, coming east. The gorge is perhaps the most sensuously beautiful part of the massif, and is the route to the Cistercian monastery from the outside world. Frequent short tunnels through precipitous cliffs keep the road close to a series of waterfalls—God's original multi-media show. The vegetation, predominantly pine trees, keeps changing in detail as if to accommodate the easily bored. Anyone who doesn't respond to this sensational five-mile stretch just doesn't like scenery.

Today's leisurely drive proves to be as easy as a stroll along the Riviera, which is where we're headed. From Grenoble at the south end of the Massif de la Chartreuse, the N85 is signposted to the southeast all the way and the traffic is not, in the off season, bumper-to-bumper. This is the old Route Napoléon, which the emperor, on release from exile on Elba, took in triumph from Golfe-Juan. Frank and I, making the journey in reverse, are not thus honored, but the increasingly warm and sunny skies make us wonder why the Great Man didn't just stay put.

As we drive south towards the Alpes-Maritimes, the rolling hills begin to look more like the Provencal scenery we're accustomed to from the paintings of Van Gogh and Cezanne: bare brown hills punctuated by thirsty scrub trees fighting for their lives. At Barréme we leave the Route Napoléon for the N202 which heads east through a series of valleys to Madone d'Utelle, where it turns abruptly south along the Defile du Chaudan towards the coast.

I was never enthusiastic about spending much time on the Côte d'Azure. My previous visits to Provence taught me to stay inland, out of sight of the Mediterranean, along which man's strutting peacock impulses have largely destroyed everything of beauty. As soon as we join the major road along the confluence of rivers which lead into the Var, the urban sprawl begins: an endless ugly snake of roadside businesses which could be anywhere in the uncivilized commercial world.

When we reach the coast and turn east towards Nice along the promenade des Anglais (named in honor of the upper-class English who, from the mid 18th century, began to shape its present character), the evening rush hour is well underway. We crawl past endless rows of medium-high-rise hotels and apartment houses, all imposing but none distinguished. What in the name of Michelin are we doing here at this hour without a hotel or any idea of where to find one? Any place within sight, if it deigned to accept us, would wipe out our assets just tipping the bellhop.

At the Mt Boron lighthouse there's a sign indicating the N7 to Monaco. What the hell—in for a penny, in for a bankruptcy! As the road climbs the side of a ridge overlooking the water, the urban sprawl thins out and we're driving through open unspoiled countryside above the intricate, discreetly developed coastline of Villefranche and Cap Ferrat. Not a cheap vulgar building in sight. What we need is a crummy hotel just around the bend on that next jutting promontory, commanding an uninterrupted 180-degree view from Nice to Monaco.

And there it is, announced by a faded sign flanked by two giant Coke bottles: L'OASIS–HOTEL–RESTAURANT–BAR. The hotel, old and weather-beaten, is low and squat where it faces the road, but sprawls two more levels down the hillside to a roughly fenced yard where a large bored dog summons up the energy to bark at a bird. To the left at upper ground level is a large covered patio with tables and chairs, overlooking a view which couldn't be bettered from any of the villas sparsely sprinkled on the hillside.

What's this dump doing here? It reminds me of friends in La Jolla who occupied a sprawling beach-side shack in the midst of a row of luxury condominiums. But this hotel has no neighbors near enough to be offended. We discover later during an after-dinner stroll that it must have a long history; there's a stop for a local bus—one per hour—bearing its name.

The patio's sensational view is shared with the dining room. The only occupied table contains a party of four which includes the *patronesse* and the chef. The latter could be the son of the former but it's obvious that, unless this is a particularly degenerate family, he isn't. They're arguing vehemently but intimately with an ease born of long practice. I clear my throat. She turns towards us and instantly replaces her scowl with a simpering grimace.

—*Bonjour, messieurs.*

—Do you have a room with two beds?

—Yes indeed.

—How much?

She brings out a grimy card listing the rooms together with their sleeping capacity and price. I select the cheapest double at 280 francs.

—May we see it?

She takes us outside, through the front door of the hotel and down a narrow, irregular flight of stairs to an ample though somewhat shabby room which looks out in the direction of the water. Prehistoric toilet and bath facilities are across the hall.

Untended trees partially obscure the view. If I had opted for a slightly more expensive room on the upper floor we would have had a panorama worth a small fortune. But what difference will it make when we're asleep? If we want to look at the water we can go upstairs and sit on the patio. That's my attitude towards travel: splurge on the meal, stint on the bed (I've a tolerant back). I put my money into things that happen while I'm awake, which is why I never buy expensive opera tickets.

It's too late to go looking for the perfect restaurant, so we take our chances. Nothing on the menu looks exciting. Frank opts for a bowl of minestrone and a plate of spaghetti. I'm intrigued by the paella at 180 francs for a double portion.

—How long will it take, Madame?

—About half an hour, Monsieur.

A good sign; it's freshly prepared.

—Good, I'll take it.

—But it's for two.

—That's OK, I'm pregnant.

Half an hour later a huge platter arrives which proves to be more a risotto than a paella, with steaming creamy round rice, hunks of chicken and fresh tuna, and a generous quantity of big shrimp, all suffused with a noticeable odor of parmesan. Not an authentic representative of any national cuisine whatsoever, but very tasty. So far as I'm concerned, the chef and the *patronesse* can do anything in private they want to. When she comes to collect the dirty dishes she exclaims over my empty platter, not realizing that the ever-obliging Frank has given me generous assistance. It was a big helping, but it was all I'd had to eat.

Mamas and *restaurateurs* are always flattered by enthusiastic piggery. Once in a Paris restaurant when I ordered a *bouillabaisse* for two (the minimum), the *maitre de* practically nominated me for the Guinness Book of Records.

L'Oasis, sur la Moyenne Corniche R.N.7, Quartier St-Michel,
6230 Villefranche-Sur-Mer

Nice Saturday October 12

The coast between Nice and Monaco is too perfect to be real. It's one of those areas like Sun Valley in Idaho or the Seventeen Mile Drive in California, where a sort of super-capitalist residents' association has succeeded in setting up an arrangement among themselves which keeps anyone from building anything so vulgar as to lower the tone of the neighborhood. Unlike the gross over-development of Cannes, there is nothing in these hills to suggest that things are not pretty much as God had left them. The villas blend unobtrusively into the countryside, with no gaudy colors or architectural excesses screaming out to call attention to themselves. Like James Bond villains, the seriously rich can make themselves invisible.

Summer weather has returned to the coast so resolutely that we can get out the shorts and sandals we'd optimistically packed in the bottoms of our suitcases. We're meeting Frank's friend Robin at the opera house in

Nice at one, so the morning is free for sightseeing. The guide books suggest that the old fishing village of St-Jean-Cap-Ferrat has kept a lot of its character, so we head down towards the water through the tiny twisting streets of Villefranche. As we come out onto the Cap Ferrat peninsula, the route is lined with the walls and gates of formidable estates, with few houses visible from the road. Hooking down towards the water, we come into the modest main street of St-Jean, lined with neat ordinary little shops selling ordinary things—a pharmacy, a Spar grocery store, a tobacconist, a news agent. No tourists yet at this hour, but the super-rich, in shorts and sandals just like us, are out for an early stroll, perhaps to pick up a newspaper or a pack of cigarettes or a bottle of Dom Perignon for their morning bucks fizz.

The road U-turns sharply to the left and brings us down to the waterfront, where hundreds of pleasure boats of all sizes—mostly large—are tied up at rows of docks. Along the other side of the street, tucked in under the backs of the shops along the street above, is a row of tourist restaurants whose menus, closely resembling each other, reflect the wide availability of frozen seafood especially shipped in from wherever in the world it happens to be cheapest. [An unfair dismissal, as I was to learn on a later trip. This is where Waverly Root ate the greatest *bouillabaisse* he found on the Riviera, and the Voile d'Or is still dishing them up.] I realize that one thing I hadn't seen along the business street was a fresh fish shop. But what does it matter, so long as the trucks are still rolling?

A couple of the mega-mansions on Cap Ferrat are now permanently open to the public. Part of the estate of King Leopold II of Belgium, the first on the peninsula to tie up his yacht in front of his own chateau, has been converted into a zoo. (In the words of Dorothy Parker, how could they tell?) Then he built a villa for his personal priest, which was snapped up in the roaring 20s by Somerset Maugham who, in *Rain*, had famously written of another disreputable cleric. We choose to visit the peninsula's most impressive temple of self-indulgence, built early this century by the demure but iron-willed Beatrice Ephrussi de Rothschild, who "commanded flowers to grow during the Mistral". Her rose pink toy box—named *Ile de France* in memory of a happy ocean voyage—is a museum of childish amusements: collections of porcelain animals, tons of bric-a-brac, priceless antique doll's house furniture which she put to use as little doggy beds, and acres of themed gardens, including a somber Romanesque grotto and a ship's prow in which parties were served by waiters in sailors' uniforms. Her personal writing desk had once belonged to Marie-Antoinette. Let them eat *bonbons*. . . .

Nice's old opera house is on the promenade des Anglais. We find a parking place only a couple of blocks away near the sea and are at the box office by one. For lunch, I'll suggest L'Acchiardo, which the Eyewitness guide to Provence recommends as "one of the few authentic bar-restaurants left in Old Nice", noted for "Nice's best *soupe de poisson*". One o'clock comes and goes, then one-thirty, then two. Frank and I decide to give Robin until two-fifteen and then take off. Two-fifteen arrives; still no Robin. He had a business appointment earlier in the day; perhaps it proved too important to terminate.

Frank has a suggestion.

—Since Robin hasn't showed up, maybe we could skip lunch and just get some bread and cheese.

—No way! I've been tasting fish soup for an hour. Go find yourself a stale crust and I'll meet you at the van. No, wait! If we have lunch, we can skip dinner and have bread and cheese tonight.

Satisfied after a moment's reflection that this might be cheaper than going to dinner, Frank rejoins me and we set out towards Vieux Nice. Our way leads through the flower market, an exotic paradise of rare blossoms. Once in the old town, I ask a shopkeeper where the restaurant is located. Behind me I hear a yell. There are Frank and Robin embracing like long-lost friends, which indeed they are. Nice, we hadn't realized, has two opera houses, and Robin had specified the new one. Deciding we might have gone to the old, he has met us by accident only a block away from the restaurant. Now tell me there isn't a God!

At almost two-thirty, L'Acciardo is just about to close, but the waitress finds us a table in back near the kitchen. The choice of fish soup is automatic, but the main course is more problematical. There are no fish courses on the menu, strange for a restaurant offering fish soup. After some hesitation I decide on *entrecote au poivre*, a dish served ad nauseam all over the world with bottled sauce, but worth a gamble at a promising bistro.

The *soupe de poisson* arrives in generous bowls, with the requisite *rouille*, grated cheese, rounds of dry *baguette*, and a dish of peeled fresh garlic cloves.

—Do you know how to eat it, monsieur? asks the pretty waitress.

I haven't encountered the fresh garlic before, but I make a shrewd guess and, using the dry bread as a grater, scrape the garlic back and forth. I start to drop the crouton into the bowl.

—Non, monsieur, you must make ze boat!

She takes the bread from my hand (brushing against my fingers!), piles on a spoonful of *rouille*, and then sprinkles the gruyere on top and places it carefully in the bowl.

—Voilà, monsieur! You may now go to sea!

She is lovely. I am afloat on oceans of desire. She can grate my garlic any time.

The flavor is up to the theatrics: a thick, rich soup, with a proper palette of flavors, and a strong garlicky *rouille*, both fully as good as the best Mary and I make at home. The entrecote is even more surprising. I had specified *bleu*, and it comes as rare as I could wish, a full half-pound, over half an inch thick, crusty with cracked peppercorns on the outside and translucent in the middle, but tender enough to cut with a fork. The sauce, rich and concentrated, has gone through all the proper stages of deglazing and reducing. Two classic dishes classically prepared and modestly priced. So far, five lucky days. Can this continue?

Out of the restaurant by a quarter to four, we've just time to visit the Matisse Museum. The drive up to Cimiez, an ancient Roman administrative center in its own right but now a fashionable hillside suburb, brings us into a splendid area of ancient buildings and parks. In front of the Matisse Museum is a large grassy space protected by shade trees. Families are gathered with *le pique-nique* spread out on blankets; children are playing, dogs barking. It's *Sunday in the Park With George*! Circled around the edge are bronze busts of classic American jazz players: and there's the Duke, jovially presiding over it all. How else could you get a statue of a nigger erected in the heart of rabidly racist Le Pen country?

The Matisse Museum is itself a wonderful exemplum of painterly deception, a 17th century villa with a *trompe l'oeil* façade whose ornate decorative stonework flattens into mere paint as you approach it. The entrance is an illusion as well. It takes us a couple of minutes to work out that the museum is entered around the corner and down the hill in the new annex.

There's only an hour and a quarter to closing time at 5:15, so we must be quick. I work my way along the walls, ignoring the need to make intestinal space for the food and wine I consumed at lunch. At a quarter to five, the lights are switched off and on several times, and at five to five, the attendants circulate, requesting us all to leave. According to the guide book, they're closing fifteen minutes early! I ask a guard the location of the WC and am told I'm too late.

—*C'est necessaire!*

I spot the logo and duck through the door as the guard hurls abuse. He follows me in and switches the light on and off, still shouting, but I'm safely locked in a cubicle. I take my time. . . .

When I emerge a few minutes later he jeers and gives me a round of applause. I assume a stately pose (easy, given my dimensions) and deliver my carefully prepared speech:

—*Monsieur, vous n'êtes pas gentil!*

Purple with rage, he hurls a diatribe as I stroll out of the building.

After dropping Robin at his hotel we explore further into the hills above Nice. The N7 to Monaco, on which the Oasis Hotel is located, is known as the Moyenne Corniche. Higher up in the hills is the Grande Corniche, which sweeps around Mont Gros to the Observatory and then back to parallel the coastline. In spite of the magnificent views there is very little building up here. How is it that, despite a notoriously corrupt Mafia-controlled city government which lasted for decades, this priceless vista has remained uncluttered, while upright local councils in northern climes dispose of their geographical dowries as fast as their suitors can sign the checks?

As we drive through the Col d'Eze around a low hill, a Magic Mountain looms in the early evening dusk. It rises up perhaps a third of a mile from the low land near the sea, but from the Grande Corniche it is slightly below us, so that we seem to be approaching it by helicopter. The ruined castle at the top makes it appear derelict, but as we draw closer we can see that there are occupied buildings clinging densely to the sides like locusts to an ear of corn. There below us now is the access road from the bottom, full of cars and pedestrians.

The Magic Mountain proves to be Eze, a *village perché*—one of the small fortified mountains, such as Mont-Saint-Michele and Les-Baux-de-Provence, which were built for protection during the middle ages. They became economically unviable during the nineteenth century and therefore derelict; but, like so many picturesque locales, they have since been resuscitated by the usual sequence of artists followed by tourists. As we walk slowly up the narrowing street, shops and houses appear to loom up out of solid rock. The street becomes a walk, then a narrow defile between buildings. Occasionally it forks, one half going downward again on the opposite side. (This, we would learn, was to confuse invaders.) As we ascend, the tiny streets, beginning to darken between the high buildings, are not crowded. Frank and I separate and there are moments when I seem to be wandering alone in a dream. The path broadens to accommodate a little patio, where an outdoor restaurant is serving temptingly fragrant meals. What a shame I suggested that this be a bread-and-cheese evening! At street level, every building is commercially utilized to the hilt, but there are no rubbishy tourist shops or vulgar signs: only art, antiques and pottery, offered so diffidently as almost to escape attention. Not a single fast food joint in sight! Who had the power—and the restraint—to maintain this site in such taste and decorum? Confronted with its magic I must stammer into silence. . . .

Frank and I meet near the top, where the path suddenly opens onto a large paved square in front of an eighteenth century church: pale ochre pedimented façade with two square white Corinthian columns superimposed from top to bottom on either side; broken-pedimented entrance and odd kidney-shaped window in the center; square lantern-tower belfry to one side at the far altar end. The doors are open and we are struck in the face by a wildly baroque interior, façade piled on façade, culminating in an improbable tiny Doric Greek temple.

A service with a congregation is in progress. It appears to be a wedding, but only because a young man and woman are standing together near a side altar. They are in simple street clothes; the priest is dressed in a business suit and clerical collar. There is no choir or organist, but some sort of canned clerical Musak is playing. The service, if it is a service, seems conversational and off-hand, as if the priest were improvising in a John Cassavetes film. The music ticks along and suddenly changes tempo in the midst of what may be a prayer; no one is kneeling, but the priest's head is slightly bowed. Frank and I watch for a while and then stroll back down through the narrow streets, which seem to have been retroactively rendered a bit surrealistic. We are indeed in a foreign country.

L'Acchiardo, 38 rue Doite, Nice ☎ 04 93 85 51 16

La Garde-Freinet Sunday October 13

On the way out of Nice, we intended to visit two more shrines of modern art, the Fondation Maeght above St-Paul-de-Vence and, next door in Vence, the Matisse-decorated Chapelle du Rosaire. The latter is open to the public only on Tuesdays and Thursdays, so we will start early at the Maeght and then take in St-Paul itself, another *village perché*, before heading down the coast.

The Maeght's museum proves to be, like the Ephrusi de Rothschild villa, a very personal collection—but what a difference in vision and intellect! The Maeghts were astute art dealers in Cannes who gambled heavily on modern artists and won handsomely, both in money and in friendship. Their collection of prime works by Chagall, Matisse and Miro served as the nucleus for a unique museum which commissioned big outdoor spaces from Giacometti and from Miro, whose Labyrinth is a complex garden of twisting paths and large playful sculptures. Braque and Bonnard were friends, enthusiasts, and contributors. The foundation has issued a prize-winning CD-ROM which takes you for a walk around the galleries and gardens, and includes both the moving image and the splash of Artigas' and Miro's witty phallic fountain, Gargoyle. I'm looking forward to reliving a delightful morning. What will today's Steptoe-and-Son art dealers leave us, other than piles of visual pollution which must be disposed of along with the agri-chemicals and atomic waste?

The Maeght collection has proved to be too absorbing to allow us time for St-Paul-de-Vence, so we head down the coast. Today has confirmed my impression of the Côte d'Azure. West of Nice, most of the family silver has been melted down; to call what is left German silver would be an insult to the *les Allemands*. Contrary to advice, we decide to skirt the shore towards Marseilles for as long as we can bear it, partly to take in museums at Antibes and St-Tropez.

Westward along the coast from Nice is blinker country: when you see something beautiful, you must restrict your vision so as to shut out the ugliness around it. Much of the road seems to have been developed by whoever got there first. Garages and warehouses jostle with garish motels and supermarkets. Only occasionally is there an open building site which, for a moment, allows you a glimpse of the eternal sea.

At the tip of the Cap d'Antibes, the old town is too tourist-attracting to replace it with condos and so on this mild October day we are still able to explore the cobbled streets and absorb the ancient ambiance. The Chateau Grimaldi by the waterfront was used as a studio by Picasso just after the war and is now a museum housing many of the works whose genesis it witnessed. We arrive there during lunch, half an hour before re-opening. I suggest a further stroll around the vicinity, but Frank prefers to perch on a stone wall and wait, so I set off alone.

Just one street away from the castle is the cours Masséna, an old covered market which is just packing up as I arrive. The refuse being hosed away by men in rubber suits looks more interesting than the choice displays in most supermarts: this is a serious market, from which the Sordello Brothers obtain much of the seafood they serve at their legendary Restaurant de Bacon. A *bouillabaisse* for Sunday lunch would be a treat, but I would have to wolf it alone while Frank munched on a baguette.

Near the market is a large English bookstore; whose mere existence says a great deal about Antibes. In the window is Mirabel Osler's *A Spoon with Every Course*, which I tried unsuccessfully to get from Books for Cooks before I left London. Richard Ehrlich's copy is now so scribbled in that I must get him a fresh copy. Besides, I couldn't bear to be without it.

By the time the Picasso Museum opens, a strong wind has come up. We go through the small front foyer onto the terrace within the battlements and are almost blown away. One sculpture near the edge is a giant arrow pointing down out of the sky and we take each other's picture, posed so that we appear to be what the arrow is pointing at. Childhood is less a product of age than of attitude.

The Picasso Museum in Antibes is given poignancy by the circumstances of its foundation. During the German occupation of France, Picasso made a heroic gesture. When everyone who could was leaving, he refused a ticket, went back to Paris and took a studio on the rue St-Augustin. There he turned out some 400 works whose somber themes and colors reflect their circumstances. Picasso was not a member of the Resistance, but he was a high-profile opponent of the Nazis as far back as the Spanish Civil War, when his painting of the destruction of Guernica spoke for a generation. Those who knew him in Paris say that his courage—one might also call it arrogance—placed him in constant danger.

There is a resonating anecdote: a Nazi officer who prided himself on his sophistication came to inspect Picasso's studio and, seeing a reproduction of Guernica, asked wryly,
—Did you do that?
—No, replied Picasso, *you* did.

The Chateau Grimaldi was made into a museum in 1928. After the war, when Picasso left Paris and came to live in the area, the museum's curator invited him to use part of it as a studio. Picasso's relief at the war's end is obvious in the works he created there, many of which are light-hearted variations on classical mythology; a blue and yellow fantasy of prancing satyrs is entitled *La joie de vivre*. Today we see his extraordinarily inventive use of junk as a deliberate mark of his originality and nonconformity, forgetting that conventional artists' and sculptors' materials had become extremely scarce. He worked with what was to hand. Don't we all.

Having had enough of coastal blight, we head inland beyond Cannes on the N7. As soon as we enter the Massif de l'Esterel, the debris is swept away and we're back into unspoiled, unlittered woodland. Mountains resist spoliation better than seacoasts: they are harder to get to, they are spread out over larger areas and, up to the point of deforestation, conceal their wounds more modestly. But seacoasts are narrow strips of desirable property which exhibit their scars like facial disfigurements. Those of us who grew up by the ocean are sad when we return because the places we knew have been desecrated or made inaccessible. A happy exception is much of Cape Cod, the saving of whose vast National Seashore along its outer edge was the triumphant life's work of artist Ross Moffat and his biographer Josephine del Deo, two indefatigable Provincetown crusaders.

At Fréjus we're forced to rejoin the coastal route to St-Tropez. When we reach Ste-Maxime the road is again solidly lined with commercial properties, though somewhat more up-market. It's late afternoon and time to look for a hotel. We drive all the way around the harbor to the old town, getting lost more than once in the maze of feeder roads. The old port of St-Tropez is full of enormous yachts which shout wealth, but the *quais* adjoining it are lined with shabby tourist traps which would be at home in any depressing down-market seaside resort in Europe. We feel as if we were following in Orwell's footsteps down the road to Wigan Pier.

The Musée de l'Annonciade with its fine post-impressionist collection is closed on Monday so there's nothing for us here and it's getting late.

Remembering our earlier inland experience, we head up into the Massif des Maures in the hope of finding something both pleasant and affordable. It's growing dark and there are no hotels. We even stop at a trailer camp, prepared to endure the unendurable in the back of the van, but can find no one in the office. And then another miracle occurs and suddenly we're on the brightly lit main street of a small mountain village with a row of picturesque little shops and cafés and a modest but presentable hotel. The patron, next door in his own bar, responds to the bell on the desk and a few minutes later we've checked into a comfortable room for a mere 200 francs. God has not deserted us.

There's even a choice of eating places still serving, not to be taken for granted in a French village on a Sunday night. We can snack on a pizza or a hamburger, or we can sit down for a real meal in a promising restaurant. Frank decides to stay in the room and forage in our lunch box, so I opt for La Colombe Joyeuse, a gay little restaurant with a gay little proprietor who turns out to be Dutch: yet another French restaurant run by a foreigner. The menu offers several local specialties including a tasty fish soup (though not quite as perfect as in Nice) and a succulent venison stew over which I linger long and lovingly.

The restaurant is small and cozy. As the evening wears on, conversation reveals that the four occupied tables all contain foreigners: two English, two Swedes, two Americans and me. I learn that the name of the village is La Garde-Freinet and that it is very popular with a close-mouthed club of Francophiles who prize it for its reticence. Rather than welcoming visitors with loud and raucous entertainment, they allow them to slip quietly into the life of the community. Those who crave discos stay away because it's boring; those who want a quiet mountain hideaway come back year after year.

If you drive through Provence, this recommendation may in itself make it worth your while to have read thus far. It's the sort of information that the guide books don't contain. They may tell you what is worth seeing but not whether you'll have to stand in line for hours to see it and then fight your way through shoulder-to-shoulder. For instance, the Eyewitness guide to Provence tells us in tiny print that La Garde-Freinet is famous for bottle corks and *marrons glacés*; the Blue Guide and Hachette mention it *en passant* but don't give it so much as a complete sentence.

Having deserted the coast, I intend to take Frank to visit Ste-Philomen, a little 16th century chateau with attached 13th century Romanesque chapel, not open to the public. They're occupied by a fine American jazz bass player named Barre Philips, to whom the French government has granted occupancy for life in return for their gradual restoration. Though identified in the Michelin Atlas, the spot is hard to find unless you've been there. It's only a few kilometers from here, north to the A8 and then southwest to the Cuers exit. A morning's visit should then see us back on the A8 to Bandol, on the coast near Toulon, where I must make a holy pilgrimage to Domain Tempier for some of the world's most seductive wine. And if I can find Kermit Lynch, who lives in the area half the year, I can ask him to autograph my copy of *Adventures on the Wine Route*, one of my oenological bibles.

La Claire Fontaine Hôtel, Place Vieille, 83680 La Garde-Freinet
☎/F 04 94 43 63 76
La Colombe Joyeuse, Restaurant, David de Scheemaecker, address as
above, ☎/F 04 94 43 65 24

Arles Monday October 14

There was a loud hiccup in today's plans, followed by the gnashing of teeth. Frank discovered that he'd misread the opening times of the Musée de l'Annonciade, which is in fact open on Monday, and wants to go back to St. Tropez to visit it. A quick calculation tells me that we can "retrace our steps", as the old Blue Guides used to say, visit Barre at Ste-Philomene in the afternoon, and make it to Bandol by nightfall. But all that extra driving isn't my idea of fun.

Barre isn't reachable by phone in the morning so we set out, intending to phone him from St-Tropez. The rush hour (some poor people have to work on a Monday morning) slows us down, but we arrive soon after opening time. Frank goes inside while I attempt a phone call. The booths in front of the museum only accept cards. Inquiry reveals that this is the rule all over town—indeed, all over France. Never mind, cards can be purchased at the local post office, which is just around the corner.

I arrive to discover waiting lines approximating those which used to prevail in Moscow at Lenin's tomb. A half-hour goes by before I reach the brusque, efficient woman behind the window. Can she change a 200 franc note? Certainly not; there is a machine at the back of the hall for that purpose. I withdraw, insert my note, and rejoin the line. Fifteen minutes later I'm at the window again.

—Large or small?

Envisioning my phone call cut off in mid-sentence, I request large.

—One hundred ten francs, monsieur.

I shove a small fortune under the window and receive a plastic card. Back at the museum I made my phone call.

—This afternoon? No problem. Come for tea.

I retrieve my card and note that two units have been used out of one hundred twenty. At this rate, I have enough credits left to phone Dial-an-Opera. Is anyone interested in a slightly used French phone card at half price? Get in touch.

By the time I'm inside the museum, Frank has covered it twice over. I make the rounds on the run (don't ask me what I saw) and join him at the entrance. By now the threatening weather has turned into a steady rain. We make a dash for the van and set out for Ste-Philomene.

I've made this trip before, so I'm confident of finding Barre's rough dirt driveway. We locate the narrow D-road without difficulty and reach a wooden sign reading STE PHILOMENE→. Looking across the road where the arrow points, I find nothing familiar. There's a house nearby at which I could ask for instructions, but two loud and genuinely serious dogs have stormed the van, snarling as though they were auditioning for Hound of the Baskervilles.

By now the rain is Noah-class. I know that the private driveway I want is there—I've taken it more than once—and so I drive slowly up and down the road, peering through the rain at each break in the vegetation, convinced that enlightenment is imminent.

It is not to be. God has decided that we, along with the whole sinful world, must be punished. I give up and head for a motorway which will take us west. The weather reports promised heavy rain for the foreseeable future, so there's no point in seeking out picturesque villages or historic towns in which to drown ourselves. It's also too late to think of visiting Bandol. Hell and damnation! We'll just have to keep going until it's time to look for a hotel.

The motorway goes on forever, and so does the rain. Past Aix—no point in puddle-jumping—and on to Arles. The exit from the N113 is ambiguous; the signs to Arles disappear and we're still on the motorway. A navigator would be useful, but Frank has gone to sleep again and I'm once more balancing the Atlas on the steering wheel.

Once we've turned around there's a promising signpost, but it brings us onto a small country road with no further instructions. After several kilometers of random driving a sign to Arles miraculously appears and within a few minutes, at about six o'clock, we arrive at the outer edge of the city. Taking the first exit, we're immediately on a wide street under a continuous canopy of enormous spreading plane trees. There are lots of parking places, and signs tell us that they're legal except on market days, which this obviously is not. Just across the street, next to an Arab bar, there's a hostelry straight out of a Pagnol film. SAVOY HOTEL proclaims a rickety sign. Sure, and I'm driving a Daimler.

A hefty motorbike is parked in the small front lobby. An Arab woman (not in purdah) shows us a room with peeling wallpaper and flaking paint. I venture to turn back the bedclothes and the sheets are clean; there's no marathon race of cockroaches to the bed's inner recesses. The price, 140 francs, is not far from what we might expect at the YMCA. What the hell. It's an adventure.

On the swings-and-roundabouts graph, an el cheapo room like this opens up the possibility of a rather splendid restaurant. I go on a quick scouting expedition and discover that we're just within the edge of the old city, with a wide range of costs and cuisines. Reporting back to Frank, I find him munching on bread and cheese from the lunch box; he's decided on another night's hibernation. OK then, I'm ON THE TOWN!

The rain has let up enough for me to close my umbrella and enjoy the misty drizzle. I stroll along, idly looking at the displayed menus. Many seem acceptable, but none are compelling. Then across the street there emerges out of soft focus a brightly lit Hollywood set of a hotel, a monumental entrance with a pillared porch, flanked on one side by an imposing chapel with a stuck-on Grecian façade, and on the other an enormous restaurant, glowing with crystal chandeliers. It could be the vestigial remnant of a monastery.

Close. It turns out to be a 17th century Carmelite convent, converted [sic] in 1929 (just in time for the Wall Street crash) into the Hôtel Jules César. The menu of the Lou Marqués Restaurant—posted at the street so that the plebes might salivate in baffled frustration—announces that it is a member of the august Relais & Chateaux chain, which includes such gastronomic shrines as Robuchon in Paris and the Hotel de France in Auch. It takes only a moment to decide on an experiment. I look like Santa in mufti: shapeless cotton slacks, a turtle-neck shirt, and a loose-fitting Suffolk fisherman's smock. I stroll up to the young *maitre de* at the front door who is taking reservations.

—*Bon jour*. When does the restaurant open?

—*Bon jour, monsieur*. At seven thirty.

—Do you have a table for one?

—*Oui, monsieur*. What is your name, please?

The details are exchanged without a single haughty glance at my clothes, my beard or my floppy leather hat. I'm off for a half-hour's walk.

When I return at seven thirty the *maitre de* greets me immediately by name without glancing at the reservation book. As he takes me to my table I apologize for being inappropriately dressed and explain that when I set out I had no intention of eating so grandly. If he would prefer to hide me away at a little table in the corner. . . .

—Not at all, monsieur.

He leads me to a table immediately next to the entrance where I can see—and be seen by—everyone who comes in. I choose the *menu du terroir* at 300 francs (five courses of local specialties) and a bottle of Domain Tempier Bandol Rosé. I'm then free to turn my attention to the evening's guests. Most of the room seems to be booked for a large party of

Americans on a Grand Tour. They're all clamoring for attention and shouting across from table to table.

—If you get a waiter, hang on to him! Don't let him get away! They're scarce as hen's teeth!

They're all ordering *a la carte*, demanding translations, deciding with difficulty, and then changing their minds. In the midst of all this confusion my courses start arriving at exactly the right intervals and the right temperatures; my wine is replenished from the chilled bottle as soon as I'm within an inch of the bottom. The young waiter is dignified but affable, stopping for brief exchanges with such unhurried poise that the restaurant might have been empty. Halfway through the meal he asks politely as he tops up my glass,

—Is the restaurant too noisy for you?

I can't help laughing.

—That's the wittiest thing a waiter ever said to me!

He smiles at our little joke and turns to the next table, where a tipsy American stockbroker is loudly demanding attention.

It's been a thoroughly enjoyable meal, but in a few days I won't easily remember what I ate. Everything was perfect, nothing was surprising. It was like a speech by a great statesman on a grand occasion. When you're serving a clientele such as this, who are paying this kind of money, you don't mess around with lemon grass in the *fois gras*.

So am I disappointed? Not in the least. I've eaten an expertly prepared dinner and witnessed a great performance—as absorbing as David Story's fine play, *The Contractor,* in which a crew of workman erect a wedding marquee on stage and then take it down, chatting as they work. At the end of the meal I'm invited to have coffee in the lounge, where for 20 francs there's a small cafetière of superlative coffee and a lifetime supply of delicious *petits fours*. If I had appeared in evening dress wearing the *Legion d'Honeur*, I could not have been entertained more graciously.

Which is exactly what I tell the *maitre de*.

Hôtel Jules César, Restaurant Lou Marquès, 9 boulevard des Lices, 13631 Arles, ☎ 04 90 93 43 20 **F** 04 90 93 33 47

Laroque Tuesday October 15

Old Arles in the rain is somber but dramatic. The Arabic population is an exotic topping on a multi-layered ethnicity that goes back even beyond the Roman occupation, whose architectural presence is everywhere you look. When Mary and I were here years ago we stayed at D'Arlatan, a historic but amazingly reasonable hotel occupying a 14th century palace on the rue du Savage. Asking where we should eat, we were sent around the corner to a cheerful little restaurant run by a French *restaurateuse* where we had a first-class *couscous royale*, as memorable in its own way as last night's Cesarean opulence.

Since Frank and I drove straight to our hotel from open countryside, his only glimpse of two millennia's history has been the dash across the street the night before, so I suggest that we unfurl our umbrellas and have a quick look around. But it appears that the only footwear he's brought for the trip is open sandals. So long as the rain continues, he'll be watching windshield TV.

It's hit-the-road time, but first a phone call to Barre to apologize for not showing up.

—Gee, I'm sorry, he says, I forgot to tell you that the board came down in a wind and we haven't got around to putting it back up.

When you live in the country you don't need signs.

I've always wanted to visit the Camargue. Weather-wise, I associate it with dry polar Mistrals or torrential rain. In either case, casual tourists stay indoors. A heavy wind wouldn't be the best time to be driving a high-sided vehicle, but today's rain is OK for a slow crawl. It's settled down to a steady snare-drum-roll on the roofs and paving stones, proclaiming that it shall rain forever and ever.

My plan is to head southwest from Arles on the D970, west on the D58 to the ancient fortress town of Aigues-Mortes, and then along the coast through Montpellier and north on the D986 towards the Massif Central. But at the junction with the D58 we continue the few remaining kilometers south to Stes-Maries-de-la-Mer. This intriguing name commemorates the miraculously safe landing of the three Maries and Martha after having been cast adrift in a *barque*. Incorporating an old pagan festival, it's celebrated every Candlemas with the eating of *barquettes*, which are primitive images of the vulva. So *that's* why I love boats. . . .

For me, seacoast towns all have the same feel. You could take me blind-folded to any small village in the western hemisphere and I would know if I were close to water as soon as I opened my eyes. Stes-Maries has a central square whose squat white public buildings would be at home among the old adobe structures of Monterey. At their front is a rectangle of small streets with modest shops and a couple of ancient churches, laid out in the grid pattern which is so common in flat country. Several little grocery stores are open and, juggling my shopping bag, my wallet and my dripping umbrella, I'm able to replenish our supplies.

On the way back to the van, the Tex-Mex illusion is complete. There's a shop, then another, selling embossed boots, embroidered shirts, ten-gallon hats, and all the paraphernalia of the rodeo. It's a tourist gimmick based on the Camargue cowboys who tame the wild white horses. Their black cattle supply the bulls that fight in the arenas. The Frontier, driven out of California, has emigrated to the Mediterranean.

Agri-business as well as tourism is invading this vast wildlife sanctuary. Since World War II, half the wetlands have been placed under cultivation and the huge nature reserves which should protect them consist only of private property with no state control of its use or abuse. I suddenly realize why so much of the land we've driven through looks like rice paddies—that's exactly what they are. These flat marshlands are ideal for controlled flooding. The Camargue, one of the last outposts of coastal wilderness, is being carved up and capitalized.

Back to the D58 and across to Aigues-Mortes through still more irrigated farmland. We might be in the Sacramento Valley. These "dead waters" are being claimed by a conglomerate of Dr. Frankenfoods who are killing the wild life which the salt marshes have always supported.

I wish the Dr. Frank sitting next to me would stop complaining about the weather.

Rising up out of nowhere on this rainy afternoon, the prospect of Aigues-Mortes is unreal. I can imagine what it must have been like half a millennium ago when, approaching it on a clear day by land or sea, it rose gradually above the earth's curvature like a fleet of vessels coming into port. Before the silting up of the Rhone's mouth, the town was itself a major port. Its founder Louis IX set out from there on the Seventh Crusade. Contemporary paintings show how high the city walls must have seemed to rise above the sea and countryside.

Along the wall near the Porte de la Gardette we find the trucks and trailers of a traveling fair which has just closed. The crowds have dispersed, the rain has lessened to a drizzle. Divine protection seems to be with us again. Within the ramparts, still intact, is a miraculous square mile of mediaeval houses and a chapel built in the late 17th century for the Gray Penitents. The town's single open tree-lined square is surrounded with cafés except at one side, where stands a church even older than the 13th century town itself. Its name, Notre-Dame-des-Sablons (Our Lady of the Sands), vividly conjures up what must have been its surreal isolation. It reminds me of a visit Mary and I made long ago to St Giles Cripplegate in London, when the surrounding bomb-damaged buildings had been cleared in preparation for erecting that architectural abomination, the Barbican. We had to pick our way across mud and rubble; it seemed to be in the middle of nowhere. This old Provencal church has been more fortunate in its ultimate neighbors.

As usual the side streets—and here that's most of the town—are empty of tourists. We walk to one of the outer walls, where a gate, locked and wire-fenced, shows an endless vista of sand and silt. Just outside is a large circle of what seem to be enormous pieces of furniture like old high-sided church pews of different designs and materials, all of them enclosing benches and seats for up to a dozen occupants. I realize with a shock that it's a DIY bull ring, in which each spectator/patron has cobbled together his own vantage point. Everyone, as John Cage says, is in the best seat!

Bullfights in Provence, unlike Spain, are traditionally an unequal contest favoring the quadruped—hardly a fight at all, more a high-risk ballet in which unarmed and unarmored acrobats attempt to snatch a ribbon from the bull's horns. The bulls themselves, whose chances of survival are one hundred percent, return triumphantly year after year. If, like Spanish matadors, they were offered the losers' ears, they would be happy to make a meal of them. Unfortunately, the international tourists who now fill the big rings find this equitable sport boring, and so the victorious bull's lifespan is becoming problematical.

Back on the road along the coast and up through Montpellier we encounter yet more anonymous seaside architecture, both domestic and industrial. It's not until we begin the ascent up the D986 into the southern foothills of the Massif Central that we begin to feel once more a part of nature rather than its vicarious vandals. By the time we arrive at St-Martin-de-Londres we're back into wooded countryside.

The village itself, though next to the main road, is a time-capsule of arcaded stone buildings surrounding an 11th century priory chapel. Romanesque architecture at its best can make me look on Gothic extravagance as somewhat decadent. This chapel's interior, though restored in the 19th century, is of such classic restraint and perfect proportions as to suggest the handiwork of some mediaeval Bauhaus: nothing is lacking, nothing is extraneous. It's a place of such supernal simplicity and composure that I would make a long detour to experience it again.

St-Martin is also home to a fine Languedoc restaurant, Georges Rousset's Les Muscardins, but it's too late for lunch and too early for dinner, so we continue north along the D986 in the direction of Ganges. Soon there's a sign indicating the Grotte des Demoiselles, one of several caves in the area. We had no particular intention of visiting any of them, but outside it's still raining and an underground grotto could hardly be wetter.

The caves are behind the face of a cliff, reached by a funicular railway. We're just in time for the last party, conducted by a jovially enthusiastic guide. Not knowing what to expect, apart from a lot of dripping water, we step out onto a concrete platform opening into a narrow Gothic-like passageway covered densely with stalactites. (Stalagmites, stalactites—which stick up and which hang down? My father taught me unforgettably how to remember: stalactites have to be tight or they'd fall off.)

The corridor opens onto a balcony overlooking a Hollywood set of a cavern, vast and complex. As we continue along a concrete path, new vistas and colors open up, infinite shades of gray and blue and purple. On the other side we can gradually make out other concrete platforms with stairs going up and down, floors of them, like an exotic Gaudi opera house. But these man-made additions are carefully discreet, in the predominant gray of the caverns. It takes a while to realize how many of them there are. No health-and-safety officer has dictated that every step should be edged with aggressive orange and black herringbones. No signs tell us what we must not do or what we must look at. No hidden loudspeakers surround us with epic film music.

The guide seems so informative, good-humored and well-received that we wish we could understand him. But it's enough just to look. Every stage of the walk up and down the endless stairs brings a new perspective, a different scale. Scale indeed: at one point the guide reaches out and strikes a group of small stalactites with his knuckles and they give out clear ringing pitches like the resonators of a prehistoric vibraphone. But there is no answering echo. These caves are silent, unresonating. The sounds hang in the air for a brief moment like the musical tears in *Bluebeard's Castle*. What a visually extravagant performance of that great Bartok opera could be filmed here! If these stalactites could talk, they would speak Hungarian.

It's over an hour before we're headed down the funicular again. Between the little lectures, it has been remarkably silent. Few people have spoken and, since we were the last visitors, there have been no distant sounds from other parties. My final thoughts are of the visionaries who made this enormous space accessible without destroying its magic, choosing a route to follow such that its structure would unfold like a symphony, with continuously interrelated changes of tempo and dynamics.

On our way again, we come almost immediately to a riverside hotel where we take an ample bed-sitting room with comfortable overstuffed furniture. At 300 francs it's outside our usual budget but we saved the extra money in our dingy cell last night in Arles. Between two large comfortable chairs there's a coffee table which we promptly convert into a wine table with a bottle of Sipp-Mack Edelzwicker. A warm room and a warm stomach lead to warm conversation. We chat for an hour before dinner the way we have chatted for decades: books, films, places, operas, jokes, paintings, terrible puns, symphonies, all the things for which we have shared a long and unquenchable enthusiasm. Frank and I are at our best just talking. For us, Sartre's *Huis Clos* would be a comedy with a happy ending.

The meal, not to be anticlimactic, will have to be wonderful. It is. The rustic dining room is lined with photographs and memorabilia of Georges Brassens, the great French antidote to arrogance, snobbery, xenophobia, and reactionary politics. Imagine a folk singer with the passion of a Pete Seeger, the wit of a Noel Coward, the intelligence of a Jacques Prevert, and the good-natured *savoir faire* of a Charles Trenet. His song for De Gaulle, *Le General dort debout*, is an ironic tribute to a stubborn martinet. And here we are in Brassens' neighborhood and, virtually, in his company.

If the cuisine then was as it is now, he was indeed fortunate. The Logis de France network strongly encourages its affiliated hotels to offer a *menu du terroir*, featuring local specialties freshly prepared. Tonight's main course is something whose name I don't recognize. The proprietor laughingly grabs my arm and pulls me out into the hallway where he points up the stairs at the far wall. Glaring down at me is the head of a wild mountain goat. No, he assures me, not *that* one; he has another which has not been hung for so long. The meal is accompanied throughout by laughter, and by a local bottle of St. Saturnin Vin d'Une Nuit. Wine for a One Night Stand? It would sell well in San Francisco.

Hostellerie Le Parc aux Cèdres, 14, route de Montpellier, Laroque,
    34190 Ganges ☎ 04 67 73 82 63 **F** 04 67 73 69 85

Le Rozier Wednesday October 16

This has been a day of spectacular scenery, the unspoiled splendor of the Massif Central. Every curve of the road reveals a fresh perspective.

With three days ahead of us before the sprint up the motorway to Rouen there's time for some leisurely touring. We start with the Southern Massif route in the *AA Walks & Tours in France*. Though austere, it is a series of mountain panoramas on a human scale. It is impossible to recommend either the route or the guidebook too highly. From Ganges we go southwest on the D25 along the Gorges de la Vis. Corkscrew indeed! The river makes a virtue of indecision, twisting back and forth on itself like a schizophrenic snake. Its path is a series of great bare-sided stone circles cut below the level of the plateau, with woodlands along its bed. The most sensational is the Cirque de Navacelles, where the river practically ties itself in knots.

Back to the D25, then south along the edge of the plateau on the D9 before plunging down a wooded slope towards Arboras, where signs direct us to the St-Saturnin Cooperative Winery. This is the source of last night's bottle and not to be missed, all the more because it's become apparent that any lengthy detours for wine or food would be at the expense of an unwilling passenger. So far as sightseeing is concerned, Frank and I can agree on modern art galleries and mountain scenery. The former being in short supply in rural France, it's down to the latter.

French wine cooperatives are generally worth visiting even without a recommendation. In conservative regions with inflexible opinions—and what part of rural France doesn't fall into this category?—they have brought together growers who realize that in today's world markets it is no longer enough to produce an anonymous table wine whose only virtues are that it is cheap, intoxicating, and not instantly poisonous. For years there flowed from the Languedoc, not a wine lake, but an ocean of rot-gut for which the State paid out enormous collective sums, so that it could be distilled into unneeded industrial alcohol—less lethal than in its vinous form—or stored in mammoth tanks as a particularly virulent form of industrial waste. It's a good thing that America never came up with a similarly hair-brained scheme for underwriting its burger joints.

The Cave Cooperative "Les Vins de Saint-Saturnin" turns out to be a large modern bottling hall with a separate cellar and sales area presided over by a jolly middle-aged lady, the sort that an ad company might select to play the part in a TV commercial. There's a well-laid-out antique display case with a glass door, in which bottles of all nine of the wines currently available are identified and priced. Around the room are neat piles of shipping and presentation cases, some made fancy with hinges and clasps. It's obvious that they do a lot of business during the tourist season, including customers wheeled in by the bus-load.

I set about tasting what's available. The top of their range, a 1994 "Seigneur des Deux-Vierges" red, is a Syrah-Grenache blend which took silver medals this year at both the Concours General in Paris and the

Concours Mondial in Brussels. It fully deserved them: dark, full-bodied and complex, with an amazingly smooth finish for such a young wine. The light red "Vin d'Une Nuit" which we drank last night turns out to be a local specialty, blended from Carignan, Cincault & Grenache in varying amounts depending on the year's yield, and given only one day in the vat. The process, like so many fortuitous discoveries, is the result of an error: a cellar manager once emptied a vat prematurely by mistake.

I work my way through the rest of their offerings and end up with something of everything. All the wines taste of enthusiasm and pleasure: to paraphrase Tin Pan Alley, let a smile be your aroma. Of the St-Saturnin Cooperative, Rosemary Frank writes in *French Country Wines* (Faber) that it is "one of the most dynamic of the Midi"; Jancis Robinson, in *The Oxford Companion to Wine*, says, "The St-Saturnin Cooperative is particularly dynamic. . . ." The word gets around.

In this warm weather there's still livestock in the high pastures. We're at least a couple of weeks early for the colorful annual festival of the *transhumance*, in which the farmers who keep their sheep, goats and cattle on the high ground in the summer bring them down to lower pastures. They are decorated with flowers and ribbons and are led along traditional paths. The word is from the root which also gives us *s'humaniser*, to come down to the level of others, a ritual which intellectual journalists celebrate with equal pomp and ceremony.

Back up the D4 along the Gorges de l'Herault, another Languedoc region now producing interesting wines, and through Ganges again onto a series of D-roads which take us circuitously north through the Parc National des Cevennes to Meyrueis. The roads become vertiginous as they climb in and out of dense forests. The fall oranges, yellows and reds are at their most vivid. At one point a tiny stream gurgles over a rock and into a small viaduct under the road, close enough so that it's easy to fill our water butt. There's no sign warning us not to, and the sparkling taste of the tumbling water is delicious.

This is countryside I would happily spend days exploring. Off to the east in our atlas are miles of mountain roads with green "scenic route" lines, looking as if they had been inscribed by an aged cartographer with the palsy. Human habitation is scarce and unobtrusive. It's impossible to make a wrong turn in country such as this; every vista seems even more dramatic and harmonious than the one before it.

The *AA Walks & Tours Guide* tells us that we must stop at Meyrueis, and again they're right. They devote a whole page to it, outlining a scenic walk through the village and up into the hills. The latter falls beyond Frank's exercise quota, but the village alone is worth the stop. It's at the confluence of two streams and has always been an important market town. Narrow twisting streets open suddenly onto little squares with panoramic views of the mountainside. In the summer it's popular with tourists, but it obviously has a life of its own. Off-season, so many tourist Meccas look like ghost towns with huge rickety hotels lining their main streets like empty barracks waiting for the next war.

We continue along the D996 following the Gorges de la Jonte to where it joins the Gorges du Tarn at Le Rozier. The riverside drive still ahead of us up the D907 is perhaps the part of our journey I've most looked forward to. As I've made abundantly clear, I'm partial to mountain roads which follow water, and Charles Shere's eyes light up when he speaks of the Tarn. But first we must find a hotel.

Just across the river from Le Rozier is the smaller village of Peyreleau where we drive up an impossibly steep and narrow street to a clutch of ancient stone buildings perched precariously on a rock. Among them is an elegantly restored and modernized building with the *Gite de France* logo, indicating that there are rooms for rent. There's no one at home. A penciled note says that the owner will be back in ten minutes. Fifteen minutes go by. The note looks a bit weather-beaten. How many days has it been there? It's starting to get dark. Shall we gamble on a French hotelier's punctuality? The question answers itself. We maneuver back down the hill and across to Le Rozier again, where an unexceptional but decent two-star hotel provides an ample room with a splendid view of the river and the hill-top village we have just left.

It's time for dinner, but there's nothing promising in town. On the hotel bulletin board are slips of paper advertising restaurants. We opt for Chez Louis a few kilometers along the Tarn, which offers *Spécialités Régionales*.

It's dark by the time we arrive, but the sign is lit, with an OUVERT suspended below. We walk in and find ourselves in a small shabby entrance hall. The paper is peeling, small objects are scattered about the floor. A little monkey of a man comes out of the kitchen, rubbing his hands on a dirty apron. He is surprised to see customers at this time of year, but takes us into a room with a coal fire and a few linoleum-topped tables furnished with unmatched chairs. There's a wooden tray of something unidentifiable in front of the fire and an old bicycle leaning against the wall. A few menus, as scruffy as the furniture, are scattered about the tables.

Against my better judgment, I order *fois gras* and *confit* of duck. My fears are confirmed when the paté arrives in the form of a small cylinder, the concentric circles of the can still visible. It tastes like the *fois gras* I can buy any time from any supermarket. I remind myself not to order fancy food in crummy restaurants.

And then the *confit* arrives, and we're in another world. The aroma is heavenly, the skin is crisp and crusty, and the flesh, though it maintains its shape, could almost be eaten with a spoon. "*Spécialité de la maison*," he informs us proudly. Further conversation reveals that the curious tray in front of the fire contains wild mushrooms which he is drying. We must come back in December, January or February, he says, when he gathers the truffles.

Would we like some local cheese? He brings us a wedge of bleu, so pungent, rich and creamy that I ask him to write down the name. It is a *bleu des causses*, from caves near Peyreleau, perhaps within sight of our bedroom window.

Another wager, another jackpot!

Hotel Doussiere, 48150 Le Rozier ☎ 05 65 62 60 25
Restaurant Chez Louis, Paul Almeras, Mas de la Font, 12720 Peyreleau
☎ 05 65 62 64 39

Le Lac de Guéry Thursday October 17

Unlike the sagas of failure, which can join writer and reader in the delicious fellowship of a shared superiority, paeans to perfection may tempt the hubristic author into what is at best a pale reflection of his subject matter. Critics through the ages have agreed that Dante's *Inferno* is more hotly felt than his *Paradiso*, Milton's *Paradise Lost* more perversely majestic than *Paradise Regained*, and the shadows in Plato's cave more vividly impressed on our imagination than the humdrum reality they so tantalizingly interpret.

And so I will not retail the splendors of the Gorges du Tarn. Adopting the Ciceronian rhetorical device of *praeteritero*, I shall pass over the fact that this steep defile between two cliffs offers a rolling panorama of dense forests, jagged cliffs, and tiny hillside hamlets, some of them apparently ghost towns with no surviving means of access, whose stones have been so absorbed into their setting as to appear like trolls' encampments erupted from the solid rock. I shall likewise ignore the fact that, at the apex of a long autumn with an early frost, the hills are painted with pointillist brush strokes. It would also be unwise to deconstruct the modulating music of the river as one passes suddenly beneath the roar of a waterfall or, in a quieter passage, can barely detect the gentle murmur of the current over smooth rocks.

Don't take my word for it. Come and see. Experience while you may this anthology of natural beauty which, unlike Yosemite or Yellowstone, does not require you to wait for hours in a traffic jam until you can leave your car in the middle of an enormous field of asphalt so that you may board a bus full of shouting parents and screaming children in order to be deposited *en masse* in a sanitized "recreation area" where campers once hiked for days without encountering another human.

But be careful whom you tell. We are a tiny circle of the discerning and the discreet. When the rest of the world discovers the delights of the Massif Central, its hills will be swarming with holiday homes and the tour buses advancing in formation bumper-to-bumper.

From le Rozier our route takes us North on the D907 following the Tarn as far as Ste-Énimie. Place-names along the way such as Pt. Sublime and Pas de Souci convey something of the spirit of the area, but the empty houses across the gorge tell another story.

Back home and writing up my notes, I recall from Oliver Goldsmith's *The Deserted Village* the lines, more timely than ever:

> *Sunk are thy bowers, in shapeless ruin all,*
> *And the long grass o'ertops the mouldering wall;*
> *And trembling, shrinking from the spoiler's hand,*
> *Far, far away thy children leave the land.*
> *Ill fares the land, to hastening ills a prey,*
> *Where wealth accumulates, and men decay.*

But Goldsmith was premature: a giant organism will proliferate from these dormant nuclei. Like Eze and Le-Baux-de-Provence, they will be rediscovered and resettled by the impecunious and imaginative, to be displaced in turn by a multi-media speculator who will organize river tours in which the punters hop from riverbank to riverbank, spending their money in the picturesque little shops which await them at every quay. *One only master grasps the whole domain,* and he will preserve its history in neon and concrete.

Ste-Énimie still thrives, a dramatically situated village with narrow cobbled streets. It is named after a 7th century Merovingian princess and would-be nun who, when threatened with a forced marriage, was blessed by God with leprosy. Later cured as miraculously as she had been stricken, she settled as a hermit in a nearby grotto. God moves in a mysterious way....

The area abounds in caves like the Grotte des Demoiselles which we visited two days ago. They are by-products of the water-soluble limestone from which these hills are partly formed. The water patiently carves underground channels which then follow the shelves of harder stone until their *resurgence* into the open air, where they join and swell the River Tarn. (Has anyone written a revolutionary poem set in this fertile flood land of allegory and metaphor?)

It is strange that such beauty should inspire me to so much anger. I think it is because I have seen within a few days so many places destroyed by pleasure-seekers that I imagine how quickly these jagged mountains could be smoothed and made cozy. I see it again later this afternoon, coming into that once-wild northern area of the Massif Central, the Auvergne. The A10/A71 south from Paris through Clermont-Ferrand has brought it within range of the metropolitan area for short holidays, and the southern third is toll-free. You may feel the effect as soon as you enter the National Park of the Volcanoes of Auvergne. Many of the roads, particularly over the high parts of the mountain range, are still uninhabited and clear of traffic, but the scale of the tourist centers shows unmistakably the numbers accommodated during the high seasons.

Le Mont-Dore has been prized for its hot water springs since Roman times, but its high-profile promotion as a tourist center has taken place during the last couple of centuries. The price it has recently paid is everywhere apparent. The town is now surrounded with an urban sprawl of nondescript hotels, and its main streets are lined with huge barn-like structures which house tourists by the train-load. There is a factory-like feel about the town, as if they were not just servicing, but manufacturing the crowds which pour through it.

On one of the little side streets we pass a grocery store with fresh fruit in boxes on the sidewalk. Suddenly I am overcome with a craving for apples, oranges, bananas, tomatoes, all those fresh juicy things that our touring diet has been short of. Frank declines to come in on the purchase, which rankles, inasmuch as he single-handedly polished off the bag of home-grown apples Mary gave us when we left. I resolutely eat my solitary way through a couple of tomatoes and an orange, and am disappointed though no longer surprised to discover that they are no better than the anonymous produce I can pick up in any shop in London. Good raw foodstuffs are still to be had in France, but mostly at the serious markets which may only be open one morning a week.

It's time to find a hotel, but emphatically not here. According to the *AA Walks & Tours Guide*, a series of small D-roads follows a scenic route to the north. As soon as we leave town the roads are immediately uninhabited. After a quarter-hour's drive a hotel appears on our left beside a river. Within is a surly family who might have emigrated from the upper Appalachians. The largest, evidently the *pater familias*, growls that the hotel is closed. It's like being told that there's no room in the work house.

A few more minutes' driving brings us to a quiet, beautiful lake with no buildings in sight except a well-designed, inviting hotel, with a large porch adjoining the water. We can be accommodated both for the night and for dinner. The architecture is modern but rustic, with softly limed natural wood. A sensibly varied menu offers a seasonal selection of wild game, including a venison soup and stewed wild hare. Cuisine, view and waitress are all stunning. Life is good.

Later in the evening I go outside to get a case from the van and am confronted with the most amazing night sky I've seen since the northern lights in Iceland: thousands of stars twinkle overhead in a vast hemisphere, the way I remember them from childhood nights more than half a century ago on Cape Cod. In the flush of enthusiasm I dash inside and summon the *hotelier* to come out and look. Together we take it in, while he points out the constellations to me. It's an everyday sight to him. I learn, not astoundingly, that he is German, with a French wife, and is not only the hotelier but also the chef. A man of *elán* and versatility, another conscientious foreigner who is upholding the standards of French cuisine.

Auberge du Lac de Guery, 63240 le Mont-Dore
☎04 73 65 02 76, **F** 04 73 65 08 78

Le Lac de Guéry Friday October 18

Noting that I have reached entry number thirteen in my Gaulic journal, I'm in danger of becoming superstitious. This has been an inauspicious day. It began promisingly with a brilliant morning sun and exceptional visibility, a daylight equivalent of last night's star-studded sky—perfect weather, in fact, to take in the panoramic view from the nearby volcanic mountain, Puy de Dome.

But Frank has something else on his mind. He has become obsessed with the expenses of our tour and chooses this morning to demand an accounting. The cost per mile of running the van, which we agreed to share equally, seems excessive to him and he wants to know the *actual* cost, as if I were making a profit. I think he's comparing my figures with the cost of running a vehicle in America, which, for political reasons, is kept artificially low. I finally get furious and tell him off with a violence I've never shown him in forty years. He's shocked and hurt. I shouldn't have lost my temper.

By the time our disagreement is ended, though not resolved, it's late morning and the sky has clouded over, with a threat of rain. We set off north, soon arriving at the attractive village of Orcival, which surrounds one of the most impressive of the Auvergne's Romanesque churches. To one side of the open square beside the church is an old-fashioned cheese shop, its wares displayed on open shelves and counters. I've been looking forward to a hand-made cantal with a thick moldy crust, the sort described so eloquently by Quentin Crewe in *Foods of France* and still available in Ma Bourgogne, Georges Simenon's favorite bistro in the place des Vosges in Paris. I bought a cantal further south in a small grocery store, but it was of the tasteless commercial variety, not unlike a mediocre supermarket cheddar. Here, if anywhere, I should find what I'm looking for.

I needn't have bothered. The large wheel of cantal prominently displayed proves to be the rindless, anonymous sort I've already encountered. It's now a familiar story: if you want the best culinary specialties of any region in the world, you must travel to Paris or London or New York, anywhere but where they are made. Do you want a really good Stilton? Don't bother to feed it with port. It isn't ready to eat until it's been laced liberally with diesel fuel.

A few kilometers further north at Puy de Dome, the threat of rain is fulfilled. The drive up the steep spiral to the top is into cloud and drizzle mostly obscuring the view we've come for. The mountain top itself is closed in, with only occasional glimpses of the surrounding countryside.

But more depressing than the weather is the immediate prospect of the mountain top itself. Most of it consists of a vast parking lot for cars and buses, with a large modern visitor-center-cum-snack-bar-cum-museum on one edge. At the other side is a small further rise of open hillside with a trail leading up to the remains of an ancient Roman Temple of Mercury, "unfortunately cluttered by an observatory, masts, etc.", as the Blue Guide succinctly puts it. The cloud has broken sufficiently to restore something of the view, which is indeed spectacular, well worth the short climb to the top. Frank opts for the warmth of the museum, to which I first drive him across the parking lot. My apparently generous gesture is an unspoken rebuke. Clothed in virtue, I climb to the top alone.

Tired of organized scenery, we elect to return to our hotel—now drawing us magnetically back to what seems in retrospect to be unspoiled wilderness—by a series of small mountain roads which should avoid the well-advertised amenities of the lower countryside. Along the way signs invite us to visit Lac d'Aydat, which, we're informed, is the largest lake in the region. A widening road leads to a large parking lot on the edge of a paved lakeside viewing point with snack bar, which even off-season is full of hungry tour bus passengers. Avoiding the crowd waiting to look through the coin-in-slot binoculars, we take to the road again.

A small D-road to a summit looks promising. It narrows to a single track and climbs into dense fog. We cross a livestock grid and encounter occasional sheep who stare at us curiously. It's lonely, eerie, and a thousand miles from anywhere. I'm thankful for the fog, which has mercifully obliterated the real estate development below.

Back at the hotel, where we've elected to stay another night, we consider eating a second time in the restaurant, but decide to drive the short distance back to Orcival, where we saw a Logis de France hotel offering a *menu du terroir*. Almost as soon as we sit down, I realize we've made a mistake. A blowzy matron and dim-looking serving girl are slouched over the bar carrying on a conversation which sounds like a French translation

of a down-market soap opera. Our arrival doesn't interrupt them. A few discreet coughs later, the menus are dropped casually onto the table. I opt for something reasonably safe, a *coq au vin*. What arrives is an object I wish I could transport to a culinary chamber of horrors: a rectangular block of meat which bears no visual, olfactory or gustatory resemblance whatsoever to a chicken. It's swimming in a lake of black goo that might have been drained from the sump of a Mack truck. Truly, one of the worst dishes I've ever had, even by charter airline standards.

Aside from a further acerbic detailing of the day's disasters, there's nothing else to say. I only wish that my romantic eagerness for the Auvergne had not denied us a second day in the Gorges du Tarn. Tomorrow is the long drive up the motorway to Rouen for the concert on Sunday. After that, who knows?

Evreux Saturday October 19

This is the day of the Big Push, the invasion of Normandy, but from the other direction. The Enemy has adopted the clever strategy of forcing us onto the national autoroutes, whose tolls are so high that by the time we arrive at our destination we'll be bankrupt and unable to afford ammunition.

But the brave Resistance has destroyed most of the tollgates on the *Autoroute Centrale* south of Bourges, so we should be able to arrive in Evreux, just short of Rouen, with enough spare change for baguettes, if not for bullets. Actually, almost all the autoroute pay stations now accept credit cards, so you can breeze through with a light heart, provided you don't read the fine print on the receipts.

As we leave Clermont-Ferrand going north, the land flattens out and the scenery becomes less interesting. But this morning the drama does not lie in the landscape, but soars in the heavens. Outpacing the weather, we pass through a succession of sunny and stormy skies for which Turner and Constable would have unpacked their palettes and paintbrushes. Violent showers which swamp the windshield wipers and slow us down to a crawl give way to dazzling rain-cleared skies arced with rainbows. For one dramatic moment two concentric rainbows mark the route ahead like glowing beacons. Then dark heavy thunderclouds loom up out of the cerulean sky and we're swimming in another cloudburst.

The route is unambiguous for hundreds of kilometers ahead, so there's no need for navigation. Frank seizes the opportunity to explore an inner landscape—or perhaps to escape from my silent disapproval—and is soon fast asleep, waking occasionally to blink at the flat scenery, mutter, "Not like the Tarn . . ." and nod off again. What will his memoirs be entitled? *Journey in the Arms of Morpheus*, perhaps. (Or *I was the Prisoner of a Gastrognome?*)

As I had hoped, we've left the autoroute just southwest of Paris by mid-afternoon and are onto the N154 towards Evreux, with plenty of time to stop at Chartres along the way. Frank and I, together with Mary, were in Chartres more than twenty-five years ago, when ex-KPFA Drama & Lit Director Jack Nessel, living in Paris for a year, let us have his flat in Montmartre for a week's holiday. It was the first (upper) floor of Madame de Maintenon's palace, the sort of pad that Hollywood might take over for a poor-little-rich-girl movie. April in Paris! Never had life been so won-drous—or so wet. It would have reminded Noah of the good old days. The leather in my indestructible hand-made Berkeley sandals cracked and split. My slides showed dramatic distortions from the water flowing across the lens of my plucky little Leica. *Singing in the Rain* would have been washed out and unfilmable.

In such weather we resolutely took the train to Chartres, where the rain continued to bucket. Cold, wet and hungry, we stopped at a large empty *brasserie* near the station and ordered three omelets. This was France and they cost a fortune—they would *have* to be good. But the chef hadn't read Julia Child. They arrived tough and serviceable, the sort of leather substi-tute you might stick on the bottom of your shoe to fix a leaky sole.

The cathedral was a twilit grotto with a few somber suggestions of color in the dark windows. If Henry Adams had visited it on such a day, his enthusiasm for the great stained glass might never have reached the page. We peered at the timeless sculptures of the west porch, the great arches of the nave, the towering tombs, as if turning the pages of some ancient guidebook or watching an ill-lit Victorian magic lantern show: *shade without colour. . .gesture without motion.*

Today, a quarter-century later, Frank and I arrive during a break in the storm clouds which sends a brilliant shaft to spotlight the whole west fa-çade of the cathedral. The cleaning and restoration of the old stone, still going on at the sides, has been completed at this end and the scaffolding removed, so that from across the plaza the great soaring structure looks as fresh as Creation on the seventh day. I take a photograph to prove to Mary that Chartres in Sunlight was not a figment of my fevered imagination.

An hour to explore the inside, this time in glorious Technicolor. No wonder we are all fascinated with these anomalous products of a violent but prolific age. This consummate craftsmanship was the collective work of highly organized, disciplined and inspired stonemasons whose spiritual descendants now parade around barefoot in leather aprons with their trousers rolled up and their shoes on their heads. What happened?

Back on the N154, we reach Evreux in plenty of time for dinner. The hotel is across from the railway station and easy to find. Its bar is a local hangout, full of enough picturesque characters to provide a whole company of extras for a Pagnol movie. Matthew Brailsford, our concert road manager, has everything under control as usual and appears at the bar just as we're checking in. Since James Wood and the New London Chamber Choir will be making a photo-finish arrival for rehearsal in the morning, dinner tonight will be *trés intime*.

An hour later the three of us are joined in the dining room by American flautist Kate Lucas. She's active in the Chicago musical scene and Frank is one of Chicago's most dedicated concert-goers, so their mutual introduction is like the reunion of long-separated Siamese twins. Names fly back and forth, old concerts are remembered, forthcoming developments anticipated, until Matthew and I become mere spectators at a world-class talkathon.

The sign outside announces that the chef specializes in seafood, so I opt for my favorite pig-out, a *plateau de fruits de mer* for two, but with no first course and no dessert. A great platter arrives piled high with shrimp, cockles, whelks, oysters, clams, and half a crab perched precariously on top. I go straight for the crab and am engulfed in the strong ammonia reek of decomposing shellfish. The rest of the platter seems uncompromisingly fresh, but what of cross-contamination? Obviously I should summon a waiter and send everything straight back to the kitchen. But it's such a happy occasion. Which is more important, principle or pleasure? Betting my life, I take the coward's way out and set the crab aside to stew in its own prolific juices.

Evreux Sunday October 20

Today is our true *raison d'être*, *l'addition* that comes with the banquet, the sole (!) justification for our two-week aesthetico-gastronomic odyssey, the bottom line of our massive self-indulgence (not to mention our own spreading bottom lines). We must install five microphones, a mixer, an amplifier and two loudspeakers, and utilize them to make a small chorus and a soloist slightly louder against the stiff competition of a battery of percussion. Is it worth the trouble and expense? Are properly prescribed glasses worth their cost to a near-sighted art lover? Yes in both cases, if our fuzzy perceptions are made more precise. The tedium of our daily lives is oft relieved by spectacles.

I say we. In order to justify the cost of his extra hotel room, Frank is officially my assistant. This presents a problem. Frank has only to look at an object, and it breaks. On the other hand, if the performance space turns out to be on the fifth floor of a hall without an elevator, I'm not going to send him out for coffee while I perform the eighth labor of Hercules.

But the Fates are with us yet again. Our concert hall is in fact a set of risers in the middle of an all-purpose exhibition hall, with large doors at one end to provide access for trucks. For the first time in my life I can drive my van to the mixing position and assemble the equipment directly from an open side door. My gear is intact and Frank is off the hook.

The concert is part of Musicavoix 1996, a large annual festival of contemporary music. Evreux is definitely not a hip town—it's like mounting a John Cage Festival in Oshkosh. James Wood has brought two of his ensembles, the New London Chamber Choir and Critical Band, together with Percussive Rotterdam, for a concert performance of Xenakis' opera, *Les Bachantes d'Euripide*. For this occasion, the dramatic action has been compressed into a single-voiced narrative, accomplished with Xenakis' approval by Christian Jéhanin. The fact that he is described in the notes as one of France's leading comedians makes me wonder just what sort of slant Xenakis is taking on Greek tragedy, until it is pointed out to me, ignoramus that I am, that *comédien* in French simply means actor. Phew!

Last night the choir was singing in London. This morning they must rehearse in Evreaux. There are no scheduled flights which will allow this. And so the intrepid Matthew has scoured Southeast England and engaged the services of Aunt Rachel's Bagel, Embroidery & Airline Company to fly the entire choir over to France first thing in the morning in a pair of twin-props lent by the Hendon RAF Museum. They will take off at seven a.m. from a Kentish pasture while the cows are being milked. The choir get to wear leather helmets with goggles. They should arrive in time, providing they aren't shot down in flames by the Red Baron.

And here they are, only an hour later than scheduled, and apparently none the worse for wear. Matthew tells me that the cost of this ingenious operation was actually less than if they had come with a scheduled airline. Surprised? Have a word with Freddy Laker and Richard Branson.

After the rehearsal we're escorted to a smaller adjacent hall for a buffet luncheon. Spread out before us on a trestle table is the old pre-fast-food France: a splendid assortment of simple classic salads, cold meats that actually taste of the animals they come from, cheeses with texture, flavor and smell, endless bottles of quaffable *vin de table*, and great bowls of creme caramel and chocolate mousse, made from ingredients, not mixes. Those who have robbed us of these simple authentic pleasures must surely rotate over an eternal barbecue.

I'm very interested in how Frank will respond to this afternoon's concert. He is the quintessential opera buff. He's been everywhere, heard everything and everybody. His collection of records and tapes fills a large Chicago basement. When I told him that our musical assignment was in fact an opera, his eyes lit up. Will a one-man cast with a chorus but no sets, no costumes and a tiny orchestra fulfill his expectations? Will the muscular, aggressive percussion of Xenakis speak to a lover of the ample orchestration of Verdi, Puccini, Mozart and Wagner?

In the event, Xenakis acquires another fan. The legend of the relentless Bacchic orgy and the eternal power of Dionysus is in the composer's blood, genetically and temperamentally, and Frank is both aesthetically sophisticated and open to receive its force. Contrary to the dogma of our times, age can yet nurture wisdom. There is hope for the future of our cultural continuity when two old strangers of such radically different legacies and temperaments can still, as transmitter and receiver, share this ancient ritual.

After the concert James and the choir are booked to return to England by the same adventurous route, and we remaining few must find some place to eat our Sunday dinner. Not so easy at it sounds. My Michelin guide lists restaurant after restaurant with the depressing note, *fermé dim. soir*. The French simply do not eat on Sunday evening. But there is one exception, with two crossed spoons and forks, Le Francais, in the center of town. Having phoned ahead for a reservation, we set out to find it.

There are four of us; my van can seat three in the cab. Frank generously volunteers to crouch in the windowless rear compartment along with the equipment, so someone else is required to navigate us by means of the minuscule city map in my red Michelin guide. Kate draws the short straw. We find our way to the center's main east-west street and drive up and down it looking for our south turning. Something doesn't feel right. I pull off to the side of the road and determine that Kate is a hundred and eighty degrees out of phase—she literally doesn't know which end is up.

I know the feeling. True navigators are born, not made. Frank deserves more sympathy and less sarcasm. Years ago I gave a ride to the south of France to a tiny Japanese photographer who was going to the same international ecological conference, she as photographer, I as sound recordist. Our schedule called for driving straight through the middle of Paris in the early morning and finding a certain all-night restaurant along the way. I plunged into the labyrinth of narrow streets, my trusty old *Paris Par Arrondissement* perched on the steering wheel. Yoko offered to navigate and I, not wanting to be rude, accepted. Her eyes flicked from page to street sign and she immediately started giving instructions:

—Ahead...take third left...left now...no, is one-way, take next left...

and so on through the convoluted heart of the city without a single hesitation. She had never been to Paris, never seen the map. Not until we were eating did she confess that her Japanese boy friend was a rally driver and she his number two. Who says the Japanese haven't a sense of humor?

Le Francais proves to be a large, modern, anonymous restaurant with plastic laminated menus—exactly the sort of establishment that *would* be open on a Sunday night. The enormous variety of food on offer must certainly come from the freezer via the microwave. We select something or other which we will forget as soon as we have eaten it—neither good enough nor bad enough to be memorable. But what would the old-fashioned alternative have been on a French Sunday night? A *croque monsieur* in a dingy café? There have been moments in a strange city after a late night tear-down when I've gone down on my knees and given thanks at the sight of a golden double arch.

Tomorrow begins the second phase of our tour. Thus far, the impending concert has set the pace and the direction of travel; tomorrow there are seven days to do with as we please. Shall we race back to the south? I don't relish another week's hard driving without reliable navigation. It will also take us to a total of four thousand miles on the clock, the expense of which keeps making Frank dig for his calculator. The answer may be, not to give up completely, but to stay in the North for a couple of days and return early, even if we have to buy a new ticket. Decisions, decisions. . . .

Vergoncey Monday October 21

As I expected, Frank is happy to accept a way out of our commitment for another week. A whole ocean full of oysters would not draw him willingly down to La Rochelle and the west coast, but the coastal region around Mont-Saint-Michel and St-Malo should yield enough to justify holding him here for a couple of days before returning to London.

My last-minute research reveals a promising small detour. According to Bartholomew's *France on Backroads*, Chateau de Vascoeuil to the east of Rouen is a "...little-known chateau [which] is one of the most charming in France. Lovingly restored to become a modern art collection..." with outdoor sculpture by Braque, Dali, Leger and Calder. It's a few kilometers north on the N154, most of it a divided motorway, and then a short distance along the N15 to the D321 and a sequence of further D-roads which must once have formed a single continuous route. (I'm reminded of Watling Street, the old Roman road north from London which was once the A5, but which suburban sprawl has now broken up below Harpendon into a lottery basket of random numbers, impossible to follow.)

When we arrive at Chateau de Vascoeuil, it's lunch time and the grounds aren't open to the public for another hour, but a sign at the gate enthusiastically recommends a visit to the local church just along the road. Its chaste gothic exterior gives no warning of the riot of saints' images and votive offerings which spill out from the choir and side chapels. Though on a smaller scale, it's like the chapel of Notre-Dame-des-Anges at the top of the Massif des Maures in southern Provence, which is full to bursting with doggerel, child-like drawings and sentimental objects of every description, all presided over by an enormous crocodile suspended from the apex of the nave. I wonder for a fanciful moment if this is a preview of our afternoon tour.

My presentiment points in the right direction. Once inside the gates, there in front of us is the building we have come to see: a small but exquisite 14th-16th century chateau, perfectly restored, with photos which reveal how thoroughly it had been allowed to deteriorate. The surrounding gardens are full of sculptures by famous artists, but they seem to have been selected to exemplify their creators' most tasteless moments. Homer nods, like the head on a dashboard doggie. There's a chain sculpture by Dali with the links welded together so that—wow!—it defies gravity. Another clever bit of Dili-Dali-ing is an exact copy of the Statue of Liberty holding up *two* torches, one in each hand. Gee whiz, why didn't I think of that?! And towering above the old mill-race is somebody-or-other's enormous nude statue of a floozy, whose grotesquely exaggerated and distorted anatomical details must have been calculated to see how far the sculptor could go before he was castrated by an angry feminist mob. Exhibited next to it, de Kooning's matrons would look winsome. [Martin's composite drawing of these sculptures, from photos, is precisely accurate]

Inside the chateau itself I'm inundated by waves of Mantovani-esque Musak, which seems to have been chosen as the most appropriate accompaniment to a grand exhibition of—nothing. There are acres of large canvases carelessly painted over with washes of bland pastel colors, with titles and a few details indicating that they were perhaps intended to be developed into paintings. On the upper level are more of the same, plus a winding staircase into a tower, promising escape. I spiral up its interior to a small circular room at the top and find myself staring straight into the eyes of an aristocratic Frenchman in velvet, lace and powdered wig, seated at a desk with books and papers before him and wearing a triumphant expression, as if he had just thought of a *mot juste*. I must have stumbled into a far-flung annex of Madame Tussaud's. In fact, a sign on the desk tells me, I am in the study of Jules Michelet.

Jules Michelet, Karl Marx's John the Baptist! The great French historian to whom Edmund Wilson devoted the first forty pages of *To the Finland Station*! And this little jewel-box of a chateau is where he spent the last years of his creative life. God must really loathe Communism. He has locked one of its greatest prophets in his own study for all eternity, hemmed in by a hell of empty art and vapid music, its window sills littered with dozens of dead flies. By now, the message will have reached him that original sin is inexorable and that his faith in the perfectibility of man was overly optimistic.

Along a path by a stream is the Musée Michelet, a tiny ancient outbuilding crammed with books, paintings, photographs and memorabilia. The omnipresent Musak makes me want to go back to the van for my earplugs. My attempt to find Frank another museum of modern art has produced a mildly amusing farce. We look at our watches and agree that it's time to move on.

There's only half an afternoon left for a long drive. Fortunately it's mostly by autoroute, the A13 between Rouen and Caen, and then the N175 down to Mont-Saint-Michel. This part of France is well covered in Alastair Sawday's self-published *Guide to French Bed and Breakfast*, so the next couple of nights would be an ideal time to make use of it. This is a guide which has never let me down. It's full of country farmhouses which rent rooms and serve dinners for bargain prices, often making use of ingredients which they produce themselves. The meals I've had at these bastions of French country cooking would have sent Elizabeth David back to write another volume.

Close to Mont-Saint-Michel near Vergoncey, declares Sawday, is La Ferme de l'Etang,

> *A beautiful house in a romantic setting next to a large lake and a chateau. . . Wonderful old varnished staircase and banister-rail, and excellent meals served next to a large fireplace in the lovely dining room.*

All this for 190 francs for B&B and 75 francs each for dinner, including wine. A phone call from an autoroute rest stop assures us of a room reservation, but no dinner; the couple who run it are out for the evening and their daughter is home alone. However, there's a hotel restaurant a few kilometers away at which she will be happy to make a reservation.

Where the motorway runs out at Caen, the road narrows to a two-lane crawl. The N175 carries a lot of traffic through hilly country, so passing is almost impossible. Instructions in the book for reaching the farm are explicit. The N175 widens out again to 4 lanes and our exit is clearly marked. But darkness is almost upon us by the time we leave the highway and it's hard to read the rural signs. We're finally at the farm by eight. There's just time to get to the hotel before the chef removes his toque. We only glance at our room, which is large and comfortable—it must be the best bedroom in the house—and are out again, racing for our dinner.

On the D998 in St-James (*St James??*) is the Hotel Saint-Jacques (that's better), an archetypically old-fashioned bourgeois establishment with massive dark furniture, walls of an unidentifiable color, and a carefully handwritten menu. Searching unsuccessfully for an explanation of the village's English name, we find in an old Blue Guide a recommendation of this hotel and its restaurant dating back to the 1950s. This will be the right place for *civet de lievre*, jugged hare. It comes as black as the oak table, garnished with mushrooms and little onions and accompanied by golden brown roast potatoes. A bottle of robust Madiran floats it gently down the gullet.

By the time we leave, the road back to the farm has been closed off for midnight repairs. We pretend that we are French and ignore the signs, driving straight through to where the road is dug up. Bouncing over the rubble, we wave at the workmen, who grin and wave back. It's big open country. There's room for everybody.

La Ferme de l'Etang, B. & J.-P. Gavard, Boucéel, Vergoncey,
   50240 Saint-James ☎ 02 33 48 34 68 **F** 02 33 48 48 53
Hotel Saint-Jacques, M. & Mme. Lemesle, 49 rue de la Libération, 50240
   Saint-James ☎ 02 33 48 31 01

Vergoncey Tuesday October 22

Children of all ages love castles in the air. Is it some racial memory of the threat of marauding hordes? Is it the power of looking down, master of all you survey, which is said to give demagogues dreams of flying over their subjects, arms outstretched? Whatever the reason, Snow White is carried off to her airy destiny, Dorothy to her land of Oz, Jesus to the right hand of God. The *villages perchés* which survived from the middle ages, such as Eze which we visited in Provence, have become terrestrial fantasylands where tourists climb the cobbled streets in search of magic.

The impulse goes back even further than Mont-Saint-Michel itself. For almost a thousand years this has been one of the most famous shrines in northern Europe and a magnet for holy journeys. The church was ever ingenious in turning secular impulses to sacred ends; wanderlust was sanctified through adoration. "Folk long to go on pilgrimages," Chaucer tells us, and gives us a vivid account of what festive occasions they must have been. When the pilgrims arrived at Saint Michael's Mount, whether in Cornwall on in Normandy, they would demand lodging, food and entertainment. The winding streets up to the holy places would have been lined with merchants catering to every level of taste and fortune.

And so it is today. Frank and I drive out along the breakwater which now gives 24-hour access and are directed into a vast parking lot which could accommodate the Rose Bowl fans on New Year's Day. It's almost empty, but a couple of school busses have already arrived. A short walk to the drawbridge, and we're inside the walls on the already crowded Grande Rue. The tariff at the grand hotels, their glass doors protecting their patrons from the riffraff, reflects the price of real estate, which rises higher into the heavens than the mount itself. But no tourist Mecca in the world is too aristocratic to accommodate a row of snack bars serving the same glop you were offered yesterday or the day before, a thousand miles away.

The only escape is upward, so Frank and I continue to the pay-point, where we learn that guided tours in various languages are available but not compulsory. We opt to proceed immediately on our own. With clever tactics, we can elude the enemy.

We don't often hear about the great architectural failures of the middle ages—those with the power to build also wrote the official histories!— but more than one bishop was heard to mutter, "Back to the drawing board."

From its very beginnings under Abbot Hildebert, Mont-Saint-Michel was a monument to *hubris*. Rather than flattening the top of the island, he constructed his great Romanesque church at the highest possible level, building out to the west and east to accommodate a nave of seven enormous bays and a great choir. It was strong enough to support the modest Norman front, but when his successor 150 years later replaced it with an all-singing, all-dancing Gothic façade with two great towers, it was too much, and between 1300 and 1600 it slowly began to come apart at the seams. Finally in 1776 (contemporaneously with the American Declaration of Independence!), three bays were pulled down and the surviving, more modest 18th century façade erected. The eastern extension lasted until the mid 15th century, when it fell during the English wars and was replaced with a florid Gothic choir finished in 1521. The adjacent abbey, justly called the Marvel, is a three-floor late Gothic extravaganza completed within sixteen years! And so the church and its environs represent half a millennium of ecclesiastical styles and values which coexist more gracefully than today's urban architecture erected within the span of a lifetime.

Frank and I arrive at the nave at the same time as a school party. Like the Viet Cong, we soon discover that one can learn the rhythms of a rigidly organized army and cut across them. Ducking down a staircase, we find ourselves alone in a fan of interlocking barrel vaults which was designed to support a part of the great weight overhead. If viewable from above, the pattern would be utterly predictable, but as we move among them, the columns interrelate in receding layers of endless complexity. This is pure Romanesque form, the sort of structured repose which, according to Henry Adams, appeals to those who have passed through the "aspirations and ambitions" of the Gothic and have "come back to rest". If he is correct, I'm even more ancient than I had feared. I prefer to believe that it appeals to me on the same plane as the uncluttered perfection of the best of the Bauhaus with its stripping away of what is superfluous, or the ultimate Zen-like simplicity of a Ludwig Wittgenstein: "Whereof one cannot speak, thereof one must be silent."

At lunch time in these lower levels we have the place to ourselves. We wander backwards and forwards, disregarding the intended route, and find ourselves, still alone, in a room housing the great treadmill which wound supplies up the mountain side. Crawling inside, I assume a working position while Frank takes my picture. I must return with proof that these three weeks were not just idle pleasure.

Along a stone corridor is a massive empty reception hall, I clap my hands, and the reverberation continues for about seven seconds. The Berkeley trombonist Stuart Dempster once played against the fourteen-second reverberation in the papal chapel at Avignon, and the tour technician—who shall remain blessed for all eternity—captured a wonderful hour of improvisation in which Stuart built sonic structures out of successive single notes, each slightly softer than the one before, so that sequences of chords, some isolated and some overlapping, were left hanging in the air. Ever since, whenever I find myself alone in a great hall, I can't resist the urge to attempt a raucous vocal imitation. I pray that St. Michael himself will not meet me at the Pearly Gates and turn me away for having desecrated his holy place.

The land west of Mont-Saint-Michel is identified in the Michelin Atlas as *polders*, a Dutch word taken into French meaning land reclaimed from the sea. It's like a miniature Camargue, flat marsh land looking out to the bay. To the east is the narrow harbor formed by the mouth of the Selune; to the west is the long hook of land jutting out into the ocean and ending at the Pointe du Grouin. Along that sandy coast is our next port of call—Cancale, whose shores have been producing highly prized oysters for two millennia. As we drive along the coastal road, the side away from the water is lined with shacks, warehouses, shops, restaurants, cafés, all piled high with oysters. Such incredible riches! It takes me back to my childhood on Cape Cod, when my father took me clam digging at early morning low tide. We would tiptoe across the wet sand looking for tell-tale bubbles. Spotting signs of life, we would dig fast and deep with our clam rakes–like gardening forks with their four long tines bent at right angles–racing to snatch the elusive mollusks out of the sand before they burrowed down too deep to be caught.

Oysters, however, lead a sedentary life, attaching themselves to rocks or to the sea bed. French oysters, being hermaphroditic, don't need to go anywhere. They just lie there, spewing out fertilized eggs and waiting to be eaten. So an oyster fisherman can bide his time, waiting for the best specimens to reach maturity. If you were imaginative, you could form a relationship with an oyster, particularly if you were yourself taciturn by nature. Which is said to be an attribute of the Breton fishermen.

Demonstrating remarkable self-control, I wait for my first oysters until we arrive in the middle of Cantale at the Port de la Houle, where we can park by the lighthouse next to a couple of benches. This is the business end of town, where the fishing boats come in. Frank is not exactly turned on by the sight of a quivering bivalve, so I get to guzzle a dozen all by myself, bought from a stallholder down by the water who splits them open and lays them out on a small plastic tray (taking care not to spill the juice) along with a wedge of lemon and a short knife for freeing the flesh from the lower shell. A dozen Cantale oysters for 18 francs! There are restaurants that add a zero.

I could easily eat my way through another dozen, and another. (There have been lotharios who devoured them by the gross on the grounds that they were potently aphrodisiac. I suspect that all those women were just an excuse for the oysters.) But there's a country dinner waiting for us at the farmhouse tonight and I like to spread my pleasure around, so we hit the road.

Down through the centuries St-Malo has lived off trade and piracy. Jacques Cartier, the "discoverer" of the St. Lawrence River whom I learned about in the fourth grade, sailed from there. The great European explorers discovered various parts of the world in much the same sense that they discovered treasure-bearing ships with foreign flags. Pragmatic precursors of Bishop Berkeley, they believed that property did not really exist until they had laid eyes and hands on it. Once they had run up a flag, it was theirs. Ever since Adam and Eve set out to label all the creatures in the Garden of Eden, the world's coasts have been littered with metal plates declaring that this or that all-conquering navigator has hereby claimed it for his monarch and named it after himself.

The D201 hugs the coast out to the Pointe du Grouin and then back past a series of tiny harbors and high coastal viewpoints to St-Malo's old walled city. It was very heavily bombed during World War II, but you'd never know it. Unlike the surrounding urban anonymity, the restoration within the walls has been integral and of a high quality—it's probably tidier than it's been since the last English bombardment a couple of centuries ago. Inside the magic circle, away from the blocks of hotels, it's one of those rich city centers which succeed in living off tourism without sacrificing their architectural or cultural identity. In a tiny square we pass a time-capsule café in which two old mariners from Central Casting are sipping their beer over a game of checkers. Trade and piracy may still be the principal industries, but now they are practiced discreetly on the punters.

By the time we've strolled about the old city, the rush hour has begun. The route back to our farmhouse is simple: down the N137 to the D4, then southeast to join the N176. But we reckon without the usual suburban ambiguities of route identification.

—Straight ahead, says Frank, looking at the map.

—Nonsense! I retort, taking the next exit.

To my silent embarrassment, Frank was right. Suddenly we're in stationary traffic on the coastal road west to Dinard. To compound our confusion, Saint-Malo is at an edge-point in the Michelin Atlas where our route must be triangulated among three pages.

—South to Dinan, Frank declares, peering through his magnifying glass. That will get us to the N176.

After a long crawl the sign to Dinan appears and we follow it. An eternity passes, very slowly. Then a crawl through Dinan and finally on to the N176.

—Dol is our destination, says Frank—then Pontorson, then Avranches.

—Avranches? Didn't we come through there last night from the other direction?

—Avranches, John. Definitely Avranches.

The road, now almost deserted, passes through a series of complicated intersections at which the builders have erected road dividers like giant pin-ball deflectors, bouncing us abruptly from one possible exit to another. AVRANCHES always appears at the last possible moment and then we have a few minutes to catch our breathe before the next frantic interchange. An hour goes by and our destination is still boldly promised, like an election pledge.

The road widens into a major four-lane highway, which begins to look familiar. Pulling over to the side, I take the atlas from Frank to find out where we are. We're miles beyond our turn-off, which was back there at Pontorson. I can make a U-turn at the next overpass and then follow the route we took last night. Together with our earlier diversion through Dinard to Dinan, we will have made two giant acute-angle detours, like the sides of a flat Christmas tree. We go into our Stan and Ollie act:

—Well, what a fine mess you've got us into *this* time!

We're still in time for dinner, thank God, and any residual ill-will is dispelled at the sight of the table. Great bowls of tomato soup, made from fresh tomatoes, are accompanied by flagons of bubbly home-made cider. The book did say wine, but I'm not complaining. Then great platters of dismembered roast chicken appear, with deep brown crispy skin, their aroma redolent of a hundred interesting things the birds had found to peck at. Every mouthful is to be savored attentively, along with the pan-roasted potatoes and the succulent broccoli. Unlabeled bottles of wine appear, making me wish I had been more cautious with the cider. But what the hell? Tonight I'm not driving.

Sharing the meal with us is a Yorkshire clan, three generations traveling together in two cars. Grandfather is accustomed to holding forth at the dinner table and we soon learn that he is one of the biggest cattle dealers in the north of England, and that his son just along the table is a dairy farmer. Our Normandy host, himself a dairy farmer of some importance, is soon engaged in a long detailed discussion of the trials and tribulations of the market. Dairy farming, he says sadly, has become an industry. In his own region during his own working lifetime, the number of independent farmers has shrunk by ninety percent. There is no longer any financial incentive to produce the carefully made old fashioned *camembert*; the craft is carried on by those who love it and can't bear to see it disappear.

Inevitably, the conversation moves on to BSE (Mad Cow Disease). Our Flying Yorkshireman tells us proudly that he's had more cattle destroyed than any other dealer, as if he deserved a medal. He has his own theories about what caused it all, and they relate to concentrated inbreeding, together with chemical treatment to control warble-fly. Nor is he sanguine about the future. He's seen early-stage BSE cattle in pastures all over Canada, he confides, but nobody will talk about it.

Our host adds that throughout Europe, farmers admitting a single case have their entire herds destroyed. He adds, with a wink, that if he wanted to ensure drastic under-reporting, that's exactly how he'd go about it.

I mention my peripheral connection with the Food Commission, a London-based gadfly which attacks the multinational food industry, and witness for the first time the spectacle of a florid Yorshireman turning pale.

—For God sake don't quote me, he babbles. No, I don't mean just by name. Don't repeat anything I've said. (He's practically on his knees.) Of course we've got it all under control now. The brain and spinal cord are all taken out in the butchering, you know.

—Yes, I reply innocently, I have tremendous admiration for those men in the abattoirs. Working at the speed of lightning, what incredible skill it must take to make certain that none of that soft tissue splashes onto the meat.

His son, silent until now, suddenly doubles up in a fit of laughter.

A platter of our host's creamy *camembert* appears, together with more wine, and then an enormous bowl of rich dark chocolate mousse. Finally, along with the coffee, another unlabeled bottle, this time a local *calvados*. Life's too short for bickering. We are all the best of friends.

Orbec Wednesday October 23

It's the home stretch—back to Boulogne and across the channel. I could do it in one day, but during the whole time we've been in France I haven't been able to visit a single restaurant in Mirabel Osler's *A Spoon with Every Course*. It's time for a ruse.

More or less on our way east, but slightly to the south, is route number five in the *AA Walks & Tours in France*, a forest tour in southern Normandy. A slow drive around half of it would bring us to Alençon, from where the route north through Rouen would take us very close to Orbec, home of *Au Caneton*, one of Normandy's gastronomic shrines. Having ascertained that they offer a bargain fixed-price menu, Frank goes along with the program. The red Michelin guide warns that table space is limited and that booking is advisable. Accordingly I ask Madame Gavard to phone for us. No problem. Immediately after breakfast we're on our way.

Today Frank is asleep almost as soon as we're on the road. But navigation is straightforward and after a few kilometers we're following the N176 signposted to Domfront, which is where we take up the AA tour. This hill town promises some spectacular scenery, which is confirmed as we approach it across a gently rolling plain. The crest of the cliff is dominated by the ruins of an 11th century castle and keep. A road spirals steeply up to it and we park nearby in the town's sleepy central square.

There is a well-manicured little park and garden surrounding the ruins, with a network of hilly paths leading to several vantage points over the plain below, and several comfortable benches, one of which Frank promptly occupies. A small patio which projects out from the edge is surrounded by a semi-circular brass plate with sighting lines identifying the features of the landscape. GARE↑ says the plate at one point and I follow the direction of the arrow to discover a derelict fan-shaped space between industrial buildings with a broad weed-grown path leading to it, which must once have been the local railway. Helpful signs for tourists shouldn't be too durable.

While I'm tracing the sight lines a wiry little old guy, wife in tow, bounces up to the parapet like a pogo stick.

—Hi, he says, as if we had just been introduced. Some view, hey?

It's the inevitable American tourist. He starts to point out features of the scenery as if he'd spent the morning memorizing the guide book. He knows this territory backwards.

—That's the later castle down there, just around to the right. That's where they hid us from the Nazis.

I've only been half listening, but I suddenly realize that this isn't just your average American tourist. He goes on to tell of being captured after the Normandy invasion, escaping with a few others on the way to prison, living precariously off the land, and finally being passed through the underground to the owner of Domfront castle, who kept him hidden, first in the castle itself and later, when that was confiscated by the Germans, in the attic of an old town house. The lord of the manor escaped detection, until one night, while his unseen guests looked on from an attic window, he was led away by the SS and packed off to Buchenwald. There, during an air raid, he miraculously escaped and ultimately returned to Domfort, where he and then his son were elected mayor virtually for life. Every ten years, on D-Day anniversary, the surviving American escapees come back for a reunion, when the mayor and the whole town treat them like visiting royalty. No phony *maquis* pretenders here. These were real heroes, and one of them is standing in front of me. I remind myself never to jump to conclusions when approached by a stranger.

Following his advice, complete with specific recommendations, Frank and I spend an hour looking around the town. The church in the center is particularly fascinating, an enormous square cruciform structure with a huge dome which is covered with a protective canopy, though there are no signs of work in progress. Unusually for a small town church in France, there is an unlocked side door, behind which there explodes a Byzantine extravaganza of metalically tinted mosaic which covers the whole complexly arched superstructure. Ornately detailed stained glass windows seem to continue the walls out into luminous space. There are places, some large, where the tiles have fallen away. Another canopy is suspended under the central dome, which must once have been a sensational climax to the whole design, but is apparently no longer safe to leave exposed; the covering outside must be there for the same reason. As we look, there is the muffled thud of another falling fragment. It's a Tower of Babel, a *fin de siècle* monument to the millennium whose ambition far exceeded its expertise. How many new follies will take shape before this century is out?

Back in the van, I try to follow the scenic route, but Frank, whom I've asked to keep track of the detailed instructions in the AA Guide, keeps dropping off to sleep at crucial moments. The only sentient creature in the cab, I lose interest in the countryside and give up trying to interpret the map alone, taking the first indicated route to Alençon, from where the way to Orbec will be signposted all the way and easy to follow.

The N138 is the old principal route from Tours to Rouen by way of Le Mans and Alençon. Orbec is a minor town off to the west on the D819, approached by way of flat country which briefly becomes hilly and "scenic" in the Michelin Atlas as you come to its edges. Its mildly interesting main street contains the picturesque flower-boxed object of our visit, then a few half-timbered buildings and, at the far end, an unprepossessing *Logis de France* hotel. It's within easy walking distance of our restaurant and looks cheap, so I go inside to inquire about a room. The bar is bustling with local characters. My inquiry brings out a large tired middle-aged woman who takes a key and plods off laboriously through the back door, up a short steep hill, and into a modern annex on an upper street. Puffing all the way, she climbs another set of stairs and opens the door of a large and obviously expensive double bedroom.

—*Combien, Madame?*

She names a figure well outside our ceiling.

—*Pardon, Madame; trop cher.*

Wearily, but without complaint, she sets off down the stairs at her shuffling pace. Eons later we are back at the bar, where she rifles through some papers and produces a dog-eared price list which includes a double room for 240 francs.

—*Tres bien*, I say, pointing at the card.

Having had her day's exercise, she summons a raw young girl who takes me to a room directly overhead. She has an aura of stale sweat so penetrating and pervasive that she must have carried it from the womb. I could have tracked her blind, allowing her a ten-minute head start, but I would have refused. Later when I park the van behind the hotel I can smell her above the diesel fumes, chopping wood ten feet away.

Au Caneton has a reputation which goes back far beyond its present young owners: almost forty years ago Elizabeth David was singing its praises in *Vogue*. So there is continuity. According to Mirabel Osler, Normandy has been able to preserve local tradition even to the point of keeping its best restaurants active outside the tourist season.

A sad footnote: Osler was traveling with her daughter and three-months-old granddaughter and comments that

> *...breast-feeding in France seems so outmoded that when Tasmin re-treated to the car* [!] *if the meal was prolonged, there was surprised reaction to such a quaint way of feeding a baby.*

What a shame that, in a country long dedicated to traditional cuisine, the most ancient and natural food of all should be so neglected!

We are greeted cordially by Madame Tricot and shown directly to our table. We needn't have bothered with a reservation; the only other diners are a young loving couple whose privacy it seems a shame to invade. I've already decided on the main course; Osler's choices were so glowingly described that to order anything else would be like doing the British Museum and skipping the Elgin Marbles. So it's M. Tricot's famous *l'aiguillette de canard au citron*.

Frank is charmed by the cozy unpretentious comfort of the dining room. Am I beginning to convert him to sybaritic self-indulgence? He's also pleased to discover that the price of the cheapest menu has dropped to below 100 francs. My emotions are mixed. All over France I've found that even the best restaurants (though not the three-star temples, which we have avoided) are now offering inexpensive alternatives at downwardly spiraling prices. The everyday competition from the cheap chains is obviously hurting. But integrity is not necessarily breached along with the 100-franc barrier. It's been very informative to eat almost every day with someone who always goes for economy, while I more or less ignore the right-hand column. Frank and I always exchange morsels, and I've discovered that his dishes are usually prepared to the same standard as my own; only the ingredients are cheaper and the recipes perhaps less complicated. But what is simpler than a perfect omelet? Just a couple of eggs, cooked in a minute from start to finish. Like a Japanese sumi painting: years to learn, seconds to do.

Here at *Au Caneton*, my point is made once more. Frank's chosen option from the cheap menu is duck, though to a different recipe. When our main courses arrive, Frank's leg of duck in a sweet and sour sauce is as interesting as my own duck breast in a sauce of lemon juice and Grand Marnier; the stronger sauce matches well with the slightly gamier flavor of the dark meat. I could happily flip a coin.

With luck, the experience will be repeatable. Osler gives the duck breast recipe, as interpreted by Shaun Hill, in *A Spoon with Every Course*. Will it travel, country to country and kitchen to kitchen? I'll include a report in an appendix.

Au Caneton, rue Grande, Orbec en Auge, 14290 Calvados
☏ 02 31 32 75 32
Hotel de France, rue Grande, Orbec en Auge, 14290 Calvados
☏ 02 31 32 74 02 **F** 02 31 32 27 77

Boulogne Thursday October 24

It's our last day of driving, a relatively easy journey northeast on the N138 to Rouen, with a stopover for lunch, then north on the N27 to Dieppe, and finally along the coast to Boulogne. To my surprise, Hoverspeed made no trouble over the altered time on our Apex flight and gave us a reservation for midnight tonight without extra charge, so there's time for a few stops along the way and dinner in Boulogne's old city.

The maze of motorways and access roads around Rouen is a nightmare. Navigation is essential. Frank resolutely unpacks his ancient Blue Guide to Northern France, opens to its quaint city map of Rouen (*Here there be dragons)* and attempts to reconcile it with the modern Michelin, an Aristotelian coming to terms with Heisenberg. Signs to the cathedral disappear and then reappear pointing in the opposite direction. In my fevered paranoia I imagine sadistic gendarmes manipulating the road signs like railway telegraphs. Suddenly, without warning—Beam me up, Scotty!— we are in a small street in the old city and a parking space miraculously empties in front of us.

Frank's historic map, now in its element, reveals that we're only a couple of blocks away from the church of St Ouen, built in the 15th century as part of a Benedictine abbey. Inside, its great uncluttered vertical lines are sublime. Not being the cathedral, and slightly off the beaten tourist track, it is of course empty. Someone is practicing on its magnificent organ, perhaps getting ready for a recording session: a pair of B&K omnidirectional microphones are hoisted high in front of it on precarious improvised stands which would have the London Health & Safety authorities turning cartwheels. The acoustic effect of the high organ's long throw—137 meters to the end of the choir—is of thunder rolling on to eternity. But according to the Blue Guide,

St. Ouen, although more uniform in style and fractionally larger than the cathedral, is a dull building in comparison, however perfect may be its architectural proportions and elaborately buttressed its soaring fabric.

Henry Adams would class this critic among the enthusiasts for the Late Gothic, impervious to the austere perfection of the Romanesque.

At the other end of the scale of restraint is the Flamboyant Gothic church of St-Maclou (named after the sixth century Welsh missionary who gave his name, in a corrupted form, to St-Malo). From its elaborately decorated portals to its renaissance glass, nothing is understated. Adjoining it to the northeast is a cloister decorated with skulls, burial implements, and all the impedimenta of a Hammer horror film, surrounding a cemetery for plague victims.

Just to the west and entered from the side by way of a small courtyard is the cathedral itself, stuffed with riches, from acres of mediaeval stained glass to the veritable Lion's Heart of King Richard himself. (Rouen appears to have been his San Francisco.) From the west portal, whose multiple portraits by Monet may have given Andy Warhol the inspiration for his most famous gimmick, the rue du Gros Horologe takes you along a row of ancient buildings, beautifully restored above, shockingly desecrated at ground level by a jam-packed concentration of tatty shops selling junk food, junk clothing, junk souvenirs, and junk music. We pass through the splendid renaissance gate with its giant clock and onward to the Place-du-

Vieux-Marché, with its modern display of junk history and junk religion. This is where Joan of Arc was burned at the stake. Her executioners should return and light their fires anew: in the center of the square is a fake mediaeval market, with an adjoining schlock-modern chapel running a continuous audio-visual show with Holy Muzak. Cecil B. DeMille would have vetoed it as tasteless.

It's time for lunch. Down a side street is an unpretentious little *crêperie* selling one of the world's great fast foods at McD-like prices. But it's still too much for Frank, who isn't all that hungry anyway; he's already polished off the *baguette* I bought for lunch this morning in Orbec. So onward to the Musée des Beaux Arts, which we discover is closed for lunch. Frank wants to wait until it reopens in two hours, but when I tell him that this would necessitate traveling on the Autoroute to Boulogne, which would cost maybe ten bucks, he's happy to set out immediately. Sigh.

Most of the coastal route is through built-up areas and too far away from the water to be scenic, but when we reach the great bay of the Somme, a side road leads off to the lighthouse at le Hourdel on the tip of the Mollières and back along the outer coast, a long straight road to infinity between rows of high hedges with a lighthouse to one side in the distance like an exclamation mark. We stop at a break on the inner side and discover that the hedge towards the water is a long row of blackberry bushes, laden with ripe fruit. What an opportunity to take Mary something she'd rather have than a Givenchy gown! I get a large plastic bowl with a tight lid from the van and set about filling it. Frank works alongside me, eating everything he picks. I bite my tongue.

With no further stops, we arrive at Boulogne in daylight. I've never had time to visit the old city, but we've four hours before our Hovercat leaves, so I drive up to the enormous St. Peter's-like basilica which dominates the skyline and find a quiet parking space under one of the great trees that line Boulevard Eurvin just outside the walls of the Ville Haute. There's time for a stroll around the old streets before deciding on a restaurant, but Frank opts out of both activities. He's decided he'd prefer to stretch out in the back of the van and sleep until we embark. So much the better. That means I can eat where I like without getting out a calculator.

After a half-hour's stroll I settle on an ancient restaurant with a some-what pretentious ambience. I'm shown to a table by a haughty waiter who's been taking basilisk lessons from the Gorgon Medusa. While I'm studying the menu, he turns to the next table and asks ritually if they have enjoyed the meal. The English wife, ignoring shushing noises from her husband, says politely that she did not think the hollandaise sauce in her first course had been properly prepared. The waiter goes into hyperdrive.

– Madame, he says peremptorily, we have served two hundred people with that dish and yours is the only complaint.

I see red. A whole day's unvoiced hostility to Frank pours over the waiter's startled head.

—The first standard by which I judge a restaurant (I announce to the whole room) is how its waiters respond to criticism. You, sir, have failed that test.

All eyes are upon me. I deliberately gather up my belongings and stalk out the door. I feel great.

Walking the streets, I think over the past three weeks. I've grown peevish and sarcastic, even abusive. I set out on the journey of my dreams, together with the friend of a lifetime, and we've fallen into the only quarrels we've ever had. Perhaps it's the secret story of many an old-fashioned honey-moon. It's the first time that we have had to live with each other's mo-ment-to-moment decisions—and spend each other's money! The devil is in the detail. A few days ago I referred to Sartre's *Huit Clos* and the pros-pect of conversing with Frank for all eternity. That's the secret: talking, not doing. Over the years, most of our time together has been spent in easy chairs.

The other restaurants on the street are either full or unpromising. Consult-ing my Red Michelin, I set off down the hill in search of one which it rec-ommends. But my tiny map is worthless in the dark. After wandering around lost for half an hour, I settle for a seedy modern tourist joint with plastic menus and a boisterous kitchen. *Moules marinière* are on the menu; they'll do, preceded by *soupe de poisson*.

—Sorry, says the waiter in serviceable English. The mussels aren't very good today. I don't recommend them. (Not much of a start.)

—What do you suggest?

—The skate wings are OK.

The fish soup arrives, a generous bowl, thick and tasty, with a good *rouille*. Then the *raie*, classically prepared *au beurre noisette avec câpres,* and a big helping of *frites*. The skate wing is huge, succulent and delicious, the capers sour and flavorful, the fries hot and crisp but smooth and creamy inside as if they'd been scooped out and puréed. It's my last meal in France, in the last place I'd ever choose. It offers hope. . .

London Monday March 3, 1997

It's now more than four months since Frank and I returned from France. During the first few weeks we exchanged a couple of vitriolic letters and then lapsed into a sulky silence.

Frank once told me a great joke about a man who gets a flat tire in the middle of Death Valley. He starts to put on the spare and discovers that he's forgotten his jack. Way off on the horizon he sees a gas station.

He sets out on the long hike. As the miles go by, he thinks to himself,
—The guy in that station will have me over a barrel. . . . He'll charge me a
fortune to borrow a jack. . .and he'll make me walk all the way back. . .and
he'll make me pay a big deposit in case I don't return it. . .and he'll laugh
at me.

As he trudges along he gets more and more furious. Hours later he arrives at the garage in a towering rage. The owner greets him at the pump:
—Hey, mister, you look plumb tuckered out. What can I do for you?

The angry sweating man hauls off and socks the garage owner in the
jaw, knocking him to the ground. Standing over him he shouts,
—I wouldn't take your goddam jack if it was the last one on earth!

Today I get a phone call. It's Frank calling from Chicago. He begins,
—About that jack. . . .
We both collapse in helpless laughter. What a silly old pair of codgers we
are! The trip of a lifetime—and then forty years of friendship gurgling
down the drain. Indeed, Frank could write his own memoir of inner rever-
ies invaded by my angry words. Returned to our senses, we enthusiastically make arrangements to meet when we're both in Vienna in a couple
of weeks.

Part 2: I ♥ RAIN

Ars June 24-30 1997

The Île de Ré's most obvious virtues are negative. Its miles of beaches are not lined with condominiums, its tourist-centered villages do not contain a single familiar fast food outlet. Even the scenery is understated. A lazy cyclist's paradise, the terrain is about as hilly as Holland. Much of it is treeless, so that after crossing its bare salt marshes a stroll through the copses which dot the periphery seems like entering the Maine woods. The buildings are uniformly low and simple, with white plaster walls and pale yellowish-orange tiled roofs. Even the traditional local pastry is deceptively austere: a *tourteau-fromage artisanal* which conceals inside its burned black tortoise-shell a soft moist cheesecake whose principal ingredient is a luxuriously high-fat *fromage frais*.

In a normal summer such visual simplicity merely emphasizes the light and the water. I had anticipated a *déjà vu* experience of Cape Cod: artists flock to such places, not because the scenery is dramatic, but because the coastal climate varies the lighting with constantly changing misty filters. Unseasonal wintry monsoons are a different matter: on this flat barren island the unhappy holiday-maker is trapped in a dour bleakness which recalls the treeless wastes near Malin Head in Donnegal or Point Reyes north of San Francisco, but devoid of their stony sweep and grandeur. If you've come here to work, you can shut the doors and windows, turn on the lights and get on with it; but if you're here for sea and sand, sun and sky, then endless sizzle-sozzle is a depressing anti-climax. It feels like a vast damp English holiday camp minus the nightly knees-up.

In such unfriendly weather there is also the psychological isolation of being trapped on an island. An impressive viaduct, almost two miles long, leads straight into La Rochelle, a busy seaport town, but the toll is a steep 110 francs. Only *to* the island of course; leaving it is free, although this summer there must be some who would gladly pay double that figure to depart.

After a ten-day soak in Paris, Mary and I approached the Île de Ré with guarded optimism. During the five-hour drive down the A10 the rain clouds had gradually cleared so that we crossed the bridge in pale wintry sunlight. Le Parasol, one of the few Michelin-recommended *Hotels de Logis* on the island which do not cost a fortune, is near the far end just beyond the village of Ars on the edge of state-protected woods. Our room proved to be at the end of a row of "studios" of the motel variety—a large bed-sitter, but with no comfortable place to sit. It contained two beds, a small round oilcloth-topped dining table with two wooden chairs and two stools (to fall between?), and that was it. No curtains, no pictures on the walls, no rugs for relief from the cold tile floors. Details were shabby; there was no bathroom cabinet, only a rough-cut shelf under the wash basin. It was the sort of austerity you might expect in a college dorm. The only modest plusses were a separate bathroom and toilet and a small kitchenette for limited self-catering. A door at the far end opening onto a private patio also admitted the noise from the main road just beyond a hedge. On a sunny day, with high holiday traffic, it would have called for round-the-clock ear plugs. At 450 francs a night we'd expected a modicum of grace. How this rated Michelin "comfortable" and "quiet situation" ratings I can't imagine. The inspector must have been a deaf mendicant friar.

After dumping our bags, we set out for a walk in the late afternoon sun through a stunted mix of deciduous and evergreen trees which reminded me both of Provincetown's "backside" and the struggling cypresses of Monterey's Point Lobos. With soft sand underfoot and twisted branches overhead, I was trudging back down the receding corridors of early childhood. As we drew near the sea, I even began to smell the evocative pungent reek of clam flats at low tide. It grew stronger. There, just across the road at the edge of the woods—could those long shallow pools be for the evaporative extraction of sea salt, an important local industry?

Nope. It was a sewage processing plant. A scene from Eric von Stroheim's *Greed* swam before my eyes, in which the loving couple share a romantic picnic on a rock by the San Francisco Bay amidst rotting fish. We turned left, then left again on a road which led back to the hotel along the edge of a sprawling trailer camp.

Putting all our eggs in one omelette, I had booked us into Le Parasol for *demi-pension*: we would be eating all our dinners there. It was the right decision. What was lacking in our accommodation was partly compensated for in the dining room and kitchen. Most of the tables were taken up every night with solid French couples who had accumulated their corporeal substance over the years in sound bougeoise establishments such as this. We would enjoy a *soupe de poisson* of robustly assertive fishiness (though the *rouille* had been toned down for effete northern tastes). There was a flawless fresh fried whole *daurade*, its complex flavors unmasked by any unnecessary and irrelevant sauce. Some of the desserts were outstanding; a myrtle tart came with a lush but not too sweet fruit filling which just managed to keep its shape without the tell-tale flavor of a floury thickening agent, perched on a crisp *pâte brisée* which tasted positively home-made. Only an occasional lapse of taste, such as a delicate fillet of *loup* whose flavor was lost in a strong grain mustard sauce, suggested that the chef was perhaps more artisan than artist. Nevertheless his dishes were consistently superior to the one meal we took elsewhere at a Gault Millau-recommended restaurant.

The first morning drowned our blue-skied optimism. We awoke to a steady rain which promised to go on forever. We had planned to bike into Ars for the daily market, but we were forced back into the van, in which we drove into town along empty narrow streets past closed shutters that made us feel like the unwelcome *avant-garde* of an occupying army.

Most of the market was mercifully indoors. It held a foretaste of infinite promise. A jovial stall-holder was selling a silver-medal-winning proprietary Bordeaux for nineteen francs a bottle. A man ahead of me, obviously a friend, sampled it and kissed his fingers to the sky. I tasted it and thought, I'm romanticizing—it can't be that good at that price. Maybe this guy is hired to encourage the punters. I finally took away half-a-dozen. I'm drinking it now. Would that I had cleaned him out!

There were yards and yards (metres and metres?) of counter space filled with unfamiliar seafood, local cheeses, spanking fresh fruits and vegetables, and a cornupopia of locally cooked dishes which, if available back home, could tempt us to lock up our kitchen and throw away the key. Their *tarte de fruit de mer* was to die for, but by the time we'd made up our minds as to just what we wanted it had sold out. We strolled along the aisles, sampling bits of cheese, salami and paté which were thrust upon us for our consideration. Everybody knew each other, and we were obviously interlopers before we had even opened our mouths—the first wave of a summer's profitable invasion.

I knew already that the excellent seafood selection was due to the labors, not of local fishermen, but of lorry drivers. It no longer comes from the harbor, but across the bridge from the huge market in La Rochelle. In a large tank at the end of the counter, *Crustacea* of various obscure species were holding a convention. The fruit and vegetables were packed in boxes which showed that most of them had traveled even further than the fish. Where today, aside from the farmers' markets of California, can you buy genuinely local produce? But there were radishes which made us care not a jot whether they had arrived from outer space: huge, crisp and hot. Even ten days later they haven't wilted—the last of them are being finished by Mary even as I write. Can radishes like that be bought in London? Perhaps at Fortnum and Mason's, in exchange for a day's wages. And there was a bin of seriously over-ripe peaches at a bargain price. For a few francs I bought a couple of huge ones with dented sides, the best of the lot, and took them back to our hotel fridge. One of them was the juiciest, tastiest peach I'd ever eaten; long afterward I was still savoring the finish of a superb *eau de vie*.

Outside the rain was bucketing down. What to do with the rest of the day? After sloshing back to our room for a cold collation, we set out for the *Phare des Baleines*, a century-and-a half-old lighthouse up which one can climb 257 steps to a panoramic view of the island. In such weather, we might even have it to ourselves.

Sick joke. We arrived at a *Via Appia* lined with rows of empty tour buses and a receding perspective of junk food establishments and souvenir shops. No international chains here—this was world-class squalor achieved entirely with local talent. The 180-foot lighthouse was flanked by giant ice cream cones in the foreground which dwarfed it at close perspective. Crowds of sullen day-trippers skulked around the shops, exhibiting evident displeasure at having been cheated out of their rightful share of midsummer sun. As we approached the entrance to the lighthouse the last of a straggle of visitors was being admitted. Without warning we were confronted with the broad oilskinned back of a grizzled guard who, Cerberus-like, barred our entrance.

—*Est-ce que possible d'entrer, monsieur?* Mary asked politely.

—*NON!* he barked without turning either of his heads.

Next we approached a shop and asked for stamps.

—*NON!* encore, with a gesture across the street.

The third response was civil but unhelpful; they'd sold out. Eager to put as much space as possible between ourselves and this Stygian vista, we splashed back to the van.

To the east from the lighthouse is a hook of land which encloses Fier d'Ars, a marshy bay in which thousands of species of birds have the official protection of a nature reserve. The road continues past the lighthouse to les Portes-en-Ré and then drops sharply south, terminating at the bay. There we found relief—not from the rain but from the tour buses. A short walk with umbrellas carefully aimed into the wind brought us to the water, which was distinguishable from the atmosphere by its slightly greater density. A sandy path along the coast through trees wound among the back yards of irregularly laid out summer homes separated by low fences and bushes. Though obviously belonging to the well-off, they were all in accordance with the prevailing white single-story tiled-roof standard. A few flowers were fighting a loosing battle with the sand and weather. There was no particular effort at security, the best protection being isolation, far from the haunts of burglars. The most boring thing about the Île de Ré must be its crime reports.

The path led back to the shore. We were the only living creatures in sight. Even the birds had sensibly tucked themselves away in whatever shelter was available. We stood braced against the wind, watching the mad *galopade* of the boats tugging frantically at their anchors. Then back to the van, back to Ars, back to the hotel, where we counted the hours to the day's climax—dinner!

St-Martin-de-Ré is the largest and most popular town on the island. In 1625 it was subjected to a long and hungry siege by the English, who thought it a very useful base to have so close to mainland France. Rescued at the last moment by a fleet of French ships—*The Alamo* with a happy ending—it was extensively re-fortified by the French master of defense Vauban in the latter part of the century.

Having successfully resisted an armed invasion, it has succumbed gracefully to the waves of tourists which inundate it every summer. Approaching through gates now wide open to all comers, we were sign-posted to the old port, a broken circle open to the sea, enclosing a central island umbilically joined to the mainland. Full of bobbing pleasure boats, it is surrounded with shops and restaurants which are picturesque and inviting. A shop-lined street leads inland from the water. Two blocks in and around a corner is an incredibly reasonable hotel which I'd seen recommended in a couple of Europe-on-the-cheap guidebooks, but hadn't dared to book. We dropped in and had a word with the cordial owner, who showed us a large pleasant double room overlooking the street, with private bath, for 270 francs. It's called Hotel le Sully. Definitely a bargain; phone/fax numbers are appended. It's on a busy street next door to a café, so take your earplugs.

Next, a leisurely tour around the shops, containing many charming, even witty souvenirs. (The city fathers should immediately be put in charge of the *Phare des Baleines*!) One store sells cheerful hand-painted pots, another is devoted entirely to things made out of wood, most of them simple and pleasing. A balancing clown pedals furiously backward and forward on a suspended string, one end of which is raised and lowered by an eccentric wheel geared to an electric motor. There's a whole cabinet full of rubber stamps which clone well-drawn images of cats and shells and windmills. They come from La Jolla, California! In a bin of kitchen implements Mary finds the wooden salad servers she's been looking for ever since we were married—complexly grained rosewood, well proportioned and finished. Another shop has my favorite fisherman's smocks in loose sturdy cotton, but with buttons up the front. Their generous cut is kind to my own generous proportions. Mary wants to buy me three as an anniversary present, an offer I can't refuse—there are few garments which fit both my own desire for informal comfort and her distaste for rampant eccentricity. My old T-shirt from Brown University graphically celebrating National Condom Week is not her idea of sartorial elegance.

The Église St-Martin is late Gothic and was once fortified. The first thing I noticed was that the entrance to the tower faces the street and is open to the public. A short stone spiral staircase takes you to a first land-ing where a verger accepts contributions for the privilege of climbing on up to the roof. Along the way, up ancient wooden stairs so narrow and vertiginous that no English Health & Safety officer would admit the pub-lic, you pass, first, the clock mechanism in a glass case, and then the three bells which it controls.

The day of our visit was miraculously warm and sunny and the view from the top gave a map-like perspective of the town. It was all so pleasant that I went down to inform Mary that it was worth the effort. On our way back up, the clock struck four-thirty and launched into an extended peal. Squeezing past the other climbers who were waiting for the noise to sub-side, I went on up to where the bells were conversing. A delicious tintin-nabulation! Poe got that word exactly right. I stayed until the first sugges-tion of discomfort (not nearly so painful as a rock concert) and then re-treated.

Every midsummer St-Martin celebrates the Feast of St John. Last year it was held on June 22nd, so we assumed that we had just missed it. Paris had celebrated the summer solstice with mega-loud amplified music until the not-so-early hours; double glazing plus earplugs only reduced it to the ominous thump of an irregular heartbeat. How salubrious it would have been to enjoy a bit of oom-pah from a village band and then retire to un-broken sleep.

A blessed miracle! In a shop window Mary spots a small poster an-nouncing the *Fête de la St-Jean*, to take place two days hence on Saturday, June 28th. A *bal gratuit* is promised, followed by a marching band to round up the citizens and lead them to the town square for *feu d'artifice* (to the music of Debussy?) and then a bonfire. We could book dinner at Les Colonnes, overlooking the harbor, where we'd just had a decent fish soup lunch, the big copper saucepan left at our table for second helpings— and then follow the band, Pied-Piper-like, to where'er it might take us.

The next morning the weather was back to its wet and windy norm. On such days the appropriate activities are eating and drinking. Now was the time to visit the Coopérative Vinicole. A brochure I'd picked up said they were open between ten and four-thirty.

According to Rosemary George's *French Country Wines*, the Île de Ré's wine-making tradition goes back to the middle ages. It was appar-ently well thought of in the late fifteenth century but its reputation subsequently declined. Nevertheless, wine is an important part of the island's economy. Along with salt, oysters and edible seaweed, grapes are still a principle harvest. The local co-op's wine was in all the restaurants, market stalls and gift shops. The white *vin de pays* called Le Royal seemed to be a universal solvent; it appeared automatically on our hotel dinner table along with the *carafe d'eau*. Its principal virtues were that it was virtually as cheap as the water and also that, after a few days, one could become accustomed to it. The fact that the vines are fertilized with the *in*edible seaweed, which, according to the green Michelin Tourist Guide, gives it "a hint of algae in the aftertaste", may tell you more than you wish to know.

Curious to learn what other wines they produced, we set out for the co-op show rooms. The journey took us to the south-eastern part of the island, in which the rapidly expanding villages were taking on an international anonymity. I could have taken photos and passed them off as Hyannis, Palm Beach, or Carmel-by-the-Sea.

The co-op factory/showroom was fronted by a parking lot designed to accommodate a fleet of tour buses. Inside were three long counters for tasting, paying and collecting. The latter two had tails of waiting customers, but the former was empty. A sign on the wall informed me that they were about to close for a two-hour lunch break—a fact which their out-of-date brochure did not include.

Picking up an inventory/price list as I left, I learned that the limited selection consisted only of the wines I had already seen on sale elsewhere. I glanced up at the large circular tower which dominated the building. It looked like an enormous barrel resting on one end. Was this perhaps the vat from which all the bottles were filled, together with an appropriate coloring agent? The Île de Ré is part of an area which until recent years could sell whatever it didn't consume locally to the distillers of cognac and industrial alcohol. Like Languedoc and Gascony, it is now being forced to produce drinkable, even distinctive wines. It's probably a tough row to hoe: flat sandy soil is not a traditional *terroir* for great vintages.

I would later discover that the local *aperitif* is, to coin a phrase, a different kettle of fish. Officially designated *Pineau des Charentes*, it is the result of combining no less than year-old cognac with new wine in its first stage of fermentation. They mature together in cask for up to five years. Quality control is certified by a panel which must approve each batch. It is made throughout the cognac region with varying success, but the *Pineau* produced by the Île de Ré Coopérative is of a high standard. It is not cloyingly sweet and achieves a satisfactory blend of its disparate elements.

In the afternoon, a visit to Loix and the "salt museum" maintained by the *Coopérative des Sauniers de l'Isle de Ré*. Passing up a guided tour in French, I made for the sales room, where salt could be purchased in more forms than I had dreamed of. My attention was immediately grabbed by *caramel à la fleur de sel*. Could this be anything like the salt-water taffy I'd grown up with on Cape Cod? Indeed it was. Who says nostalgia ain't what it used to be?

Morton's Iodized Salt used to claim, "When it rains, it pours". On the Île de Ré that applies only to the weather. Don't put their salt into a shaker. It won't come out because it is hygroscopic (there's a two-bit word!): no magnesium carbonate has been added. The most refined-looking crystals are *fleur de sel*, which is skimmed off the top during evaporation and then separately sun-cured. The dirty-looking gray salt contains useful trace elements and is recommended by *Larousse* for use in the kitchen, reserving the more elegant white product for the table.

What a lot of fuss, you may think—salt is salt. I might have agreed before I cooked with the sea salt we brought home. I found it to have a delicate flavor which made the seasoning of foods more controllable. It's easy to add just the right amount, so that the mixture neither tastes of salt nor seems to require it.

On Saturday St John intervened and the sun returned. We were able to put Plan A into operation, which was to visit La Flotte in the afternoon and then come back the short distance to St-Martin for dinner and the *fête*.

Itself an ancient seaport, genteel La Flotte allows its elder brother to be the center of attention. It is a town to live in rather than merely to visit. Its shops are more useful than frivolous. I was immediately seduced. A vintner was selling his own *blanc de blanc* straight from a stainless steel vat, decanted on demand into old plastic bottles. At only eight francs a litre I couldn't resist. The next day I would taste it from the fridge, shudder, and pour it down the drain. As the legendary *négociant* is said to have explained, "This wine isn't for drinking—it's for selling!"

La Flotte feels classically Mediterranean, but with a modest restraint which is not typically Latin. There are many streets of simple well-kept houses which are neither austere nor ostentatious. The usual pattern of white walls, green shutters and orange tile roofs prevails. The only exuberant feature is the thousands of hollyhocks which the whole island supports in such weedy profusion. These flowers seem to do well in sandy seaside soil and a damp climate (though too much rain will wither the leaves). In Provincetown the long footpath behind our house was known as Hollyhock Lane, a name which led my father to restore this striking floral feature.

In a little square tucked away amongst the residential streets is Hippocampe, a small hotel which well deserves its "modest comfort" rating in Michelin. Its 18 rooms start at an incredible 102 francs per night, but it is no shabby flea-bag. Rather, it is a modest delightful inn out of a time machine, with an enclosed garden and outdoor breakfast area. The harbor is just a couple of minutes away down a small semi-private path. If we return to the Île de Ré, the first thing I will do is to book it.

While looking for the hotel I found a gleaming white church, a Gothic jewel box. Unadorned on the outside (as a jewel box should be), its interior reveals both the prosperity and the judicious restraint of its conservators. The decoration is representative of ebullient Catholic taste, but selectively highlighted at key focal points. In the common practice of votive offerings, there are model ships hanging from the ceiling, but only a few, carefully placed and of superb craftsmanship.

The interior was totally restored in the 1980s. This involved not only repainting, but also the rebuilding of wooden structures which had partially rotted away, and even the construction of totally new features that are so compatible with the old as not to be immediately obvious. The repainting is also remarkable: it includes *trompe l'oeil* columns and draperies which are deceptive precisely because they are comparatively simple and therefore plausible. The ancient wooden pews were splashed with color from sun through stained glass. We stayed longer than in any other church on the island.

Do I sound like the La Flotte Chamber of Commerce? So be it. In my present mood I could happily live and die there.

Back in St-Martin, the *maitre de* at Les Colonnes had obligingly saved us a window table overlooking the harbor. The food was neither good nor bad enough to be very interesting, but the prospect was pleasing and the open window wafted away the cigarette smoke. By the time we had paid the bill, it was growing dark.

The sound of a marching band informed us that the *fête* was underway. They came into view, dressed in white trousers, blue jackets and yaughtsman's caps, just like the uniform I wore in the Provincetown marching band at the age of twelve. There, in fact, was a young lad looking very much like a picture Dad took of me over half-a-century ago. My eyes did not remain dry.

The musicians were accompanied by a swelling crowd of townspeople plus a few tourists, with dozens of small children bearing simple Chinese lanterns hanging from sticks and made of accordion-pleated paper in pastel colors with small votive candles in tin cups resting on their cardboard bottoms. No Eureaucrat would have given his approval, but there were no mishaps.

The band played a repetitive fanfare as it snaked through the streets, finally arriving at the Place de la Republique for the concluding ceremonies. A big bonfire, maybe twelve feet high, awaited ignition. But first there were the fireworks, not awesome by Hollywood standards but, within the context of the occasion, on just the right scale. We were close by and could observe them in detail: it was more chamber music than grand opera.

Finally, the bonfire (which God in his infinite mercy had refrained from soaking with a day's hard rain) was dowsed with petroleum and set alight. We all drew closer and then gradually fell back as the flames rose and the heat spread out. A handful of kids on the edge of the square carried on with their own little fireworks display but nobody, including the *gendarmes*, seemed worried. The square floated somewhere in time and space, absorbed in a universal small-town ritual: Norman Rockwell with a French accent. We drifted back to the van, which we'd parked just a block away beside the church, and inched slowly out of town through the happy dispersing crowds.

The next morning the rain was bucketing down with renewed vigor and the puddles around our little studio had become a moat. There were three days left of our holiday, but to what purpose? Risking a penalty for early departure, we gave notice for the following morning and immediately felt more cheerful. After all, it was only money; our time was once more our own! We paddled back to the Ars market and stocked up on salami, cheese, radishes, another Tortoise Cake and various things that would help us remember the good moments.

This was the place of which so many had said, "The Île de Ré! You lucky people! You'll love it!" But most of them have friends or family living there, to fold them into the community. I thought of my return visits to Provincetown over the years, sometimes in the dead of winter, when the lonely tourist would have fled in consternation. But there are friends waiting for me who make the weather a matter of small importance. Gazing outward from a room warmed by a log fire, a hot drink and cordial companionship is not like shivering on the street, staring in at another's pleasure. If Mary and I return to the Île de Ré I hope that next time God, at least, will make us welcome.

Le Parasol, rte St-Clément-des-Baleines, 17590 Ars-en-Ré
☎ 05 46 29 46 17 **F** 05 46 29 05 09
Hippocampe, 17630 La Flotte ☎ 05 46 09 60 68
Hotel le Scully, 17410 St-Martin-de-Ré
☎ 02 46 09 26 94 **F** 02 46 09 06 85

How pathetic! A sniveling, ungrateful report. An American composer wrote us up last year; he was much more sympatique. *The Île de Ré is My modest holiday home; if I want occasional relief from the eternal effulgence of My official residence, that's My affair. In fact, on their way back to London Mary and John were very lucky in Normandy, where I granted them beautiful scenery, sunny weather, and two extra nights in one of my favorite* châteaux. *I even allowed them three meals at Au Caneton in Orbec, where last October one of my personally trained chefs had served John and his long-suffering companion Frank a wonderful duck on their last night in France. But you'll never hear this side of the story from your pompous narrator. He'd rather play for sympathy.*

Part 3: Dining Out in Paris

...gourmets. eternally engaged in a never-ending search for that imaginary, perfect, unknown little back-street bistro....

Roy Andries de Groot

Artists, capitalists, radicals, reactionaries, intellectuals, philistines—all may come together in brief and illusory harmony over the dinner table. Trotskyists and Le Pen-Pals wax lyrical over *brandade de morue.* Such is the magnetic attraction of a really good cheap bistro that in no time it can become a mediocre assembly line, its only begetter having long since retired to the Bahamas.

For the fanatic, poverty is no barrier to gourmandizing. The artists starving between the wars in Parisian garrets scraped together their centimes for an occasional blow-out at Michaud's. The more modest cafés, frequented by habitués, bitchués and sons-of-bitchués (thank you George Stewart), became hang-outs for the affluent as soon as they were fictionalized. The final word was unwittingly said by the lady who asked a librarian for George Orwell's restaurant guide, *Dining out in London and Paris.*

Here are a few places worth considering that I visited on my last trip. Get there before a sticker appears in the window reading:

AS RECOMMENDED
IN
Through Darkest Gaul

Le Petite Niçois, 10, rue Amélle (7th) Tel: 01 45 51 83 65
Lous Landès, 157 avenue Maine (14th) ☎ 01 45 43 08 04
Le Refuge du Passé, 32, rue du Fer à Moulin (5th)
☎ 01 47 07 29 91

> *Bouillabaisse, cassoulet,*
> *Their making is not paltry play.*
> *Cassoulet, bouillabaisse,*
> *Bad victual doth the fool abase.*

Freely translated from the Langue d'oc

Bouillabaisse and *cassoulet* are two classic peasant dishes that have been promoted from "folk song" to "art song". Folk music may be handed down from generation to generation, but the songs are different every time you hear them. Although there are certain accepted conventions, each event is determined by the forces available and the inspiration of the performers: no one complains if they slip in a variation, or even make up an extra verse. So long as the tradition is maintained to a degree that satisfies the audience, the hook will not reach out from the edge of the stage.

Art songs, on the other hand, are meticulously written out. The composer is God. Not only the notes are indicated, but also the dynamics and tempos and the manner in which they should be altered. Overlaying this are further conventions introduced by those performers who are particularly revered. Sometimes these may contradict each other, and then fierce battles rage among their followers.

Ardent purists in both genres are agreed on only one thing: you do not feed the song into a sausage factory to be ground up and spit out as Musak. Barbara Allen and the Maid of the Mill both lose their virtue when they bed down with pop stars.

—But what has this to do with geese and gurnards? you rightly ask. Classic folk recipes were pragmatic solutions to particular problems. When the fishermen had disposed of their catch, what to do with the ugly little suckers that no one wanted? When the Golden Egg—the *paté de fois gras*—had been extracted for the *seigneur*, how did the farmer and his wife set about cooking their own goose?

Before domestic freezers, fish stews were the art of utilizing the ephemeral. They could be great feasts for special occasions but when you were hungry, whatever fish or shellfish you had went into the pot. (Just ask a peasant, if you can find one.) Waverley Root, in his classic *The Food of France*, devotes a dozen pages to demonstrating that "each locality [has] its own variation of the dish. . . [T]he exact constituents of any particular *bouillabaisse* may depend. . .on what the nets have brought up that day." The unsightly *rascasse* appears to be the only essential ingredient, the stone that the builders had rejected becoming yet again the chief cornerstone. Years later in his *Provincetown Seafood Cookbook*, Howard Mitcham, after hitch-hiking on a fishing boat, would proudly tell of the memorable stew he made with a mountain of "trash" fish he had snatched from the swooping gulls.

On Cape Cod we had the clambake, in which various molluscs and crustaceans were cooked in a hole in the ground (together with corn-on-the-cob, potatoes in their skins, and whatever) on a bed of stones first heated by a fire which had been built over them. On these occasions I ate lobsters with the casual abandon of a young landlubber devouring hot dogs. But we had no equivalent hodgepodge which was boiled up with fish and vegetables, except for the hot spicy Portuguese stews that were off limits to us little WASPS-in-training. It would be years before I tasted the foods whose mysterious aromas had wafted up from the kitchen down the hill.

My eventual search for the ambrosial *bouillabaisse* met with mixed success. Ten years ago Mary and I were in Provence for a heavenly week during which I spend the nights recording Barre Phillips and Barry Guy improvising on their bass fiddles in Barre's Romanesque chapel. The B&B at which we stayed served wonderful dinners, but I had set my sights on the ultimate experience. An hour's drive away over the coastal mountains at Lavandou was a Michelin-starred restaurant whose listed specialty was the sacred stew. Nothing for it but to make the pilgrimage.

Arriving in good time for lunch, we learned that their *bouillabaisse* required twenty-four hours notice. By this time I had vowed not to be defeated, and so we made the necessary arrangements and stayed on for a well-prepared but anticlimactic set menu.

The next day, another long drive over the mountains to the coast. The occasion was already marred by my admission that the cost of a *bouillabaisse* for two at this gastronomic temple was 800 francs. It had better be perfect.

It wasn't. After a long wait an enormous cauldron of over-stewed fish arrived, with large rings of tough squid and a double handful of tiny crabs, each containing about a teaspoon of meat. The broth was thin and anemic, not remotely as fishy as the *soupe de poisson* we regularly made at home. But the quantity seemed endless—Santa's sack would not have served as a doggy bag.

While my stomach was swelling to meet the challenge, Mary went off to the powder room and returned looking bemused. She had just had a surreal experience. While she was combing her hair, the waiter had entered, put his arms around her waist, and started to kiss the back of her neck. She faced the quandary of the functionally mono-lingual: a high-school French qualification had not taught her what to say to an unwelcome *libertin*. (Today such behavior even on the Riviera would probably raise his voice by an octave.) She left immediately—he offered no resistance—and returned to a meal which was scarcely more welcome. We puzzled over what to do, if anything, and were thoroughly nonplused. Our mood was not improved when *Madame* at our B&B informed us that she could have done a real *bouillabaisse* at a fraction of the price. When the scene of our *contretemps* disappeared from the next Michelin, we wondered if our wanton waiter had finally been, as it were, exposed.

Five years later, in Paris for a performance of the Berio *Sinfonia* at the *Theatre des Champs Élisées*, I tried again. This time I zeroed in on another Michelin-starred restaurant just a couple of blocks from the theater. The Big B was on the menu for 300 francs. I ordered it for the following evening.
—I am sorry, Monsieur, said the waiter, but a minimum of two is necessary. The fish are too large for only one.
A good sign. They didn't use chunks or fillets.
—That's not a problem. Prepare it for two and I will eat nothing else.
The waiter looked discreetly appreciative.
—Very good, Monsieur.
The next day I skipped lunch. By dinner time I could have devoured a raw sea urchin, spines first. The fish arrived on a platter for my inspection,

sleek and bright-eyed. There were no large shellfish. Good. To me, a crab or a lobster perched on top of a *bouillabaisse* is an excrescence. It is no more appropriate there than next to a steak, as in that American *lusus naturae*, Surf 'n' Turf. These noble *Crusacea* deserve one's undivided attention. In a cauldron fit for a feast they enrich the flavor and are not disproportionate, but in a small dish served at table they often return to the kitchen scarcely disturbed, having been placed there to show the rest of the diners that the host has a long purse. One of my fantasies is getting to know a *restaurateur* who will allow me to dine every night off the lazily-picked lobsters sent back to his kitchen.

After a suitable interval the fish returned cooked, still on the bone. They were presented again, piping hot, to show that each had been added at the correct stage. The top fillets were then deftly removed and served with a little of the liquid. The broth was robust and flavorsome, indicating that the chef had followed Root's preferred practice of cooking the fish in bouillon—fish soup, even. If the dish is made with water, as in Lavandou (unless in large quantities, with a whole phylum of fish), the broth can be anemic.

Next came the soup in a separate bowl, thick and rich. It was accompanied by a strong hot *rouille*, by no means to be taken for granted in Paris, or even Province, where it must often be requested.

One lap of the course was covered, my own lap extended. The rest of the fish, which had been kept warm in the kitchen, followed. I loosened my belt and began again. I could feel the eyes of the waiters upon me, as if they had made private wagers among themselves. There went the last morsel of fish. Then came another bowl of soup. It seemed even larger than the first. More in the tureen. Would I reach the finish line? I popped a button and breasted the tape. Thank God I'd ordered only half a bottle of *Muscadet*. No *entrée*. No *Badoit*. No desert. No coffee. No *petits fours*. But I had single-handedly negotiated the rivulets and rapids of the *Grand Bouillabaisse*. There in the bubbling current, fin-to-fin with the *saint-pierre*, the *rouget* and the *rascasse*, swam the *merlan*. The whiting had come home to spawn.

In Paris this year for a ten-day visit, my ambitions were more modest. Michelin and Gault Millau went to the bottom of the stack and up came Gaston Wijnen's *Discovering Paris Bistros* (translated from the Dutch) and Sandra A. Gustafson's unsalubriously titled *Cheap Eats in Paris*. The former, though eight years old, was new to me. The latter had been a useful companion through several editions: it led me to several of my long-standing favorites, including two Meccas for American tourists, Chez Denise and Ma Bourgogne, which nevertheless continue to attract the natives, the latter brasserie even refusing all credit cards.

Both books strongly recommended a bistro in the 7th Arrondissement which specialized in seafood: Le Petit Niçois. They agreed that its *bouillabaisse*, available as part of a 155-franc menu, was an outstanding bargain. Wijnen described its exact method of preparation in such detail as to indicate that his information came straight from the *bouche du cheval*: seven varieties of fish cut into large hunks, plus a few molluscs and crustaceans; the firmer ones marinated for several hours in olive oil with onions, tomatoes, garlic, fennel, parsley, thyme, bay leaves, pepper, orange peel and saffron; then cold water added and boiled for seven or eight minutes; then the softer fish added and cooked another seven minutes. It seemed a practical, labor-saving way for a bistro to prepare an evening's supply. But, whether kept warm or re-heated, it would continue to cook. Better to arrive early. As for the end-of-evening bacteria count, when dining out in France I rely on statistics. An equation which includes both my age and the frequency of my visits gives me an excellent chance of dying from some other cause.

On a Saturday night, a reservation was essential. It proved to be a cheerful, nautical place in blue and white. American accents could be heard from several directions. A couple at the next table had evidently been guided there by *Cheap Eats*; they too were tucking into the eggplant fritters. Dry and vaguely commercial in flavor, they proved to be a disappointment. In fact, it was superfluous to have ordered an *entrée* at all. The *bouillabaisse* arrived in a large copper saucepan full of chunks of fish, with a few small clams and half a soft-shell crab. It was not elegantly laid out, but the single portion was enough for two, at a fraction of the cost of my two Michelin feasts. The chunks came out of the pan without falling to bits, they maintained their individual flavor, and the broth was a creditable fish soup in its own right, with generous bowls of *rouille*, dry toast and the proper grated *gruyére* that goes stringy in the soup and dribbles down your chin. Available on the *à la carte* menu at under 100 francs, it's got to be the cheapest respectable *bouillabaisse* in Paris, if not in all of France. My other two courses were unnecessary, both the fritters and the *cantal*, which proved to be inferior to the ripe rindy cheese served at Ma Bourgogne in the place des Vosges. No matter. I would return to Le Petit Niçois if their fish stew were the only item on the menu.

If a *bouillabaisse* is a watercolor which must be executed with *élan*, a *cassoulet* is an oil painting, built up layer by layer and allowed to set between its successive stages. At its zenith it may become a masterpiece, like Lindsey and Charles Shere's Cassoulet for Groundhog Day in *The Open Hand Celebration Cookbook*, spread out over a week and shared each year with the same circle of friends. At the other end of the scale is the version in the London Cordon Bleu *Casseroles* cookbook which, though it includes no cans, bottles or packets, can be prepared from scratch within a few hours and is a recognizable and tasty approximation. In between are successive levels of complexity which yield increasing rewards in accordance with the excellence of the ingredients and the skill and patience of the cook.

As with *bouillabaisse*, there is no general agreement as to exactly what goes into it. According to Waverley Root, it all began in a continuously simmering *cassole* on the back of the stove, "serving as a sort of catch-all for anything edible that the cook might toss into the pot." That was possible when wood-fired stoves were constantly kept alight. Some *cassoulets* within living memory have claimed a twenty-year life span. Eighty years ago in Kentucky, when my father was a circuit-riding preacher, he was served a delicious soup by one of his parishioners. When he asked her for the recipe, she threw up her hands and exclaimed, "Lor'! There ain't no recipe for soup! It jes' *accumulates!*"

The lowest common denominator that Root found was that "...it is a dish of white beans...cooked in a pot with some sort of pork and sausage. After that it is a case of fiddler's choice." Everything depends on the fiddler. The Toulouse tradition, including preserved goose, has become the School of Pagannini, in which any substitution is regarded as anathema. Such controversies, although they seem to echo the minute doctrinal divisions which have led armies to mutual slaughter, nevertheless insure that, at certain times and places, the quality of what is served will be very high indeed, whatever school it follows. As with the making of wine, indifference as to detail leads to an indifferent product.

The first serious *cassoulet* I remember was largely wasted on me. A dozen years ago I was in Auch for a late-night concert with the electroacoustic vocal quartet, Electric Phoenix. On Sunday I escorted them all to lunch at

M. André Daguin's great Hotel de France, where I carefully nibbled my way through a *menu degustation* of Gascony specialties. The maestro himself came out from the kitchen and consulted over our collective menus. Two of our company were vegetarians and, instead of fobbing them off with something simple and boring, he inquired in detail about their likes and dislikes.

The next night after the concert we were all taken down a back street to an ancient room on an upper floor, with no sign to tell us where we were. Seated on benches along trestle tables, we drank darkly dense red wine from dusty unlabeled bottles and waited for we knew not what. After an eternity, bubbling golden-crusted pots appeared on the table and something resembling Boston baked beans with generous hunks of meat and sausage was ladled out. It was very tasty, but it seemed a bit primitive after the elegant repast of the previous day, served on fine china and rounded off with fifty-year-old *armagnac*. One day I would learn that M. Daguin was himself one of the great exponents of *cassoulet*. I would also realize that up those worn wooden stairs in a darkly beamed refectory we had been allowed to share in an ancient ritual. Like John Wesley in an upper room in Aldersgate, I felt my heart strangely warmed.

Later I would begin to make my own *cassoulet* based largely on Richard Olney's recipe in *The French Menu Cookbook*. Constructed in four stages which can be completed over a couple of days, it calls for home-made confit of goose; a bean stew made with pork rind, green bacon, a pig's foot and garlic sausage; and a lamb stew with bony hunks of shoulder, onions, carrots, tomatoes, garlic and white wine. These separate recipes are then combined and baked slowly in a pot, topped with bread crumbs and dribbled with goose fat so as to form a rich brown crust.

I'm afraid I overdo the crust. I cook the *cassoulet* in a square oven-size three-inch-deep earthenware dish so as to maximize the surface, breaking it up several times so that it continually reforms and enriches, ultimately making up a substantial proportion of the recipe. (It must, of course, be topped up frequently so that it doesn't dry out.) I have been severely reprimanded for this; it is the wrong shape of pot. I admit that overall texture probably suffers and, when a wonderful aroma fills the house, flavor can be subtracted from the final product. I hereby confess my wrongdoing. But like a good Catholic I shall doubtless sin again.

However you make it, it will tempt you to excess. Paula Wolfert's search for the perfect *cassoulet* as detailed in *The Cooking of South-West France* turns me as green as a casaba with envy. She cites Prosper Montagné, author of the first *Larousse Gastronomique*, who once came across a sign on a bootmaker's shop in Carcassone reading, *Closed on Account of Cassoulet*. The making, the eating or the recuperation? Perhaps all three.

Back in Paris for an extended visit after several years of *cassoulet* construction, I was curious to find out how it fared in a restaurant. By this time I had moved from my elegant 1st Arrondissement hotel to an even more comfortable rented room in a large top-floor apartment near the south-west edge of the Latin Quarter, for an amazing 200 francs a night. (Once again, Sawday's *Guide to French Bed and Breakfast* had made itself indispensable.) My landlady entered into my researches and recommended a restaurant just along the street.

In the end I was nudged in the direction of Lous Landès in the 14th Arrondissement by both Michelin and Gault Millau, the latter pronouncing its version "world-class". Which world? It proved to be watery, with scraps of confit, a small round hard stick of sausage that might have held a mortise-and-tenon joint together, and undercooked dry starchy broad beans. (One cookery pundit, claiming that there is progress in classic cuisine, cites as proof the fact that after the *haricot* was imported from Spain in the 19th century, the *cassoulet* was no longer made with broad beans.)

But the restaurant was modestly elegant, the service was suave and friendly, and the meal was rescued by tiny wild black olives from Nice, an excellent cream of asparagus soup, and a robust prize-winning Chateau de Diusse Madiran 1992 which, at just over 100 francs, was almost the cheapest wine on the menu. After finishing with a summer fruit *sorbet* that was as sharp and refreshing as a traditional English summer pudding, I was prepared to forgive them.

The next day I reported to Madame that my quest had not been successful. She in turn confessed that our discussion had aroused both her hunger and her curiosity, and that she had gone that same night to our neighborhood restaurant and, for the first time in years, had eaten a *cassoulet*. It was, she said, excellent. And the *ambiance*, she asserted with a wink, was *très sympatique*.

I was now under a moral obligation to sample a *cassoulet* on two successive nights. I strolled down to find the restaurant, which went under the unpromising name of *Le Refuge du Passé. Passé* indeed. Through the window I could see that the walls were covered with camp theatrical posters and curled photos of luvvies in eternal embrace. It would have made a perfect set for La Cage aux Folles.

That evening the restaurant filled up rapidly with several parties—all straight—who seemed to be anticipating an entertainment of some sort. The *maitre de*, who was as camp as his posters, greeted us all effusively. Ordering from a set menu, I started with a lentil salad topped with a lightly poached egg. Tasty. Then the *cassoulet*, obviously superior to that of the previous night as soon as it reached the table. The texture was creamy; the beans held their shape until bitten into and then dissolved; there was a generous proportion of confit; and the sausage was thick, juicy and well garlicked. No trace of crust, but that's hard to manage when it's reheated to order.

In the meantime our *maitre de* had returned and was chatting up the tables one by one, gradually pulling them into a collective farce. The skill with which he played us off against each other suggested that he must have spent years on the stage before retiring to the wings. My dessert arrived, an over-the-top dish of vanilla ice cream with syrupy *mirabelle* plums, flamed with *eau de vie*. Cloyingly rich, but appropriate to the occasion.

When everyone had been served, the chef came out and was subjected to a well-polished patter of insults from the *maitre de*. They did a Laurel and Hardy routine in which they slagged each other off, taking turns being on top. I was pulled in along with the other diners, unable to grasp the jokes but nevertheless having to respond with ambiguous pantomime that drew laughs which I couldn't interpret. It was all rather surreal but lots of fun. Everyone went away happy. Good food, amusing entertainment. It wasn't what I'd had in mind, but I wouldn't have missed it for the world.

Meanwhile, I must revisit that Upper Room in Auch before they start serving Honker MacNugget Beanburgers.

L'Ecurie, 58, rue de la Montagne Ste-Geneviève (corner rue Laplace), 75005 Paris ☎ 01 46 33 68 49

Charles Shere's *Three Weeks in Paris 1977* contains on the first page the following entry:

> *Sophie returned, then F., & we walked up Mouffetard to L'Ecurie in rue du Mont S. Geneviève for dinner [160]: we had*
>> *Salade de tomates*
>> *Paté*
>> *saucisson*
>> *selle, côte d'agneau & chateaubriand*
>> *crêpes aux poires flambé*
>>> *vin en pichet*

If I read this correctly, that was a three-course dinner for four, including wine, for 160 francs—cheap even twenty years ago. Last year Charles returned and found the restaurant unchanged except for the prices, and those had not kept pace with inflation. These are the very restaurants that are fast disappearing, and so a visit was mandatory.

I went on a sunny evening (one of the few this sodden summer) and found an ancient seedy building whose decor, inside and out, could best be described as Dickensian Hippie. The façade was the sort of black which might have begun decades ago as any other color, with decoration which included a couple of brightly-painted cartoons and an amazing tattered photo of an ancient bearded gentleman on an enormous tricycle, a parodic Horseman of the Apocalypse. Over the sidewalk hung a sign with a stylized representation of a strutting Etruscan stud. The tables inside were crowded and higgledy-piggledy, so I opted for a small table on the sidewalk in the sun with the grill just the other side of an open window. There I could enjoy everyone else's dinner as well as my own.

I was immediately brought a glass of sangria, a basket of bread, and a generous dish of aïoli which must have kept the staff occupied all day crushing the garlic. The aroma wafting through the window told me that my first course had to be grilled marinated sweet peppers and tomatoes, brushed with the marinade and sprinkled with basil. These proved to be succulent even beyond expectation. For a main course I settled on grilled lamb chops and French fries and was rewarded with lamb which tasted simply of lamb and fries which tasted of potato. My only mistake was to pass up the house wine for an indifferent Provencal rosé. Subsequently I would adopt the maxim,

Don't stray
  From the cliché,
Just stay
  With the pichet!

At the end of a leisurely meal I was brought a glass of calvados. (Like the sangria, it came with the territory.) By then the restaurant had filled up and a young couple with a baby, evidently friends of the staff, were regretfully informed that there was no room in the inn. Observing a star in the East, I stood up and offered them my table, which they gratefully accepted. Conversation revealed that he was himself a *restaurateur*, in charge of a riverside restaurant at the Bastille which was mentioned in one of my guide books. It was his night off. I was reassured; "Eat where the chefs eat," is my motto.

He proved to be very familiar with L'Ecurie and knew something of its history. The building itself, he thought, went back to the 16th century and the ground floor had been a restaurant for at least a hundred years. I would later discover that the bar inside was an original *zinc*. This was the metal from which they were usually made, so that it became the generic term even when the bar was wood or even plastic. Alas, this became common during the last war, when almost all of the zinc bars were melted down by the Germans. This is one of the few to survive, and the maker's seal is evidence that it dates from just after the Great War (as opposed to the others).

My informant went on to tell me that L'Ecurie was noteworthy for the excellence of its meat and also its *super gambas*. I would be able to verify this at lunch the following day. Not wanting to suffer the near-fate of my new acquaintants, I made a reservation for one o'clock. But first I would have to move from my luxury hotel in the 1st Arrondisement, paid for by IRCAM, the computer music research center established by Pierre Boulez—the great good place where worthy electroacoustic composers go when they die. Since I was remaining in Paris between weekends at my own expense, I opted for a B&B on the south edge of the Latin Quarter.

Back at my sidewalk table, soon to bear my name on a brass plaque, I ordered the *super gambas*. Four of them arrived on a large platter. They were are biggest king prawns I'd ever encountered; I would have hesitated to engage them, live, in single combat. Chewy and succulent, they were a meal in themselves, but were nevertheless accompanied by an enormous baked potato, which I had discovered was an optional substitute for the fries. Having chosen the low-fat alternative, I proceeded to drown it in aïoli. I'm a true American: I always drink calorie-free Badoit with my Ben & Jerry's super-rich vanilla ice cream.

As I ate my lunch an over-decorated woman of a certain age was pulled past me, as if on wheels, by three identical toy dogs on identical leashes. She had also passed by the evening before. I was beginning to feel at home.

On a roll (to coin a phrase), I booked dinner for seven-thirty that evening. I was to meet James Wood, a fine English composer with whom I've worked for twenty years. James is someone I have always bitterly resented. Possessing a voracious appetite for fiery vindaloos, he has been known to tuck into my left-overs; and yet he could model for an Oxfam poster. The explanation must be metabolic. (I refuse to accept the alternative that he simply works harder than I do.)

James had the incredible fortune of working in Paris for a month on a new piece at IRCAM. With his world reputation as a lover of good food, introducing him to L'Ecurie could guarantee its survival well into the next millennium.

I began by following James' example, a blue cheese salad. It was a simple large bowl of lettuce with a creamy blue cheese dressing, and then a surprise at the bottom, some more crumbled bits of blue cheese. This is contrary to the usual restaurant practice, which is to fill the bowl with lettuce and then put the expensive bits on top where they're visible. A whole day's crab salads may thus be gleaned from a single crustacean.

My main course was again lamb, but this time a grilled slice of leg cut straight through the bone. Both these courses plus a desert (my choice being a *cassis* sorbet packed with bits of ripe fruit), were among the alternatives in the bargain menu at 98 francs.

When was the next time I could make an excuse to return? What about the following evening, when I was to meet T. Wignesan, the Stateless Civil

Servant? (That's the title under which I've told him he must publish his autobiography.) Wignesan (who refuses to divulge what the T stands for—is it perhaps his Tantric identity?) is a research fellow in comparative literature and was a long-time friend of the late poet and scholar Eric Mottram. Friends of Eric belong inexorably to a world-wide club from which, like the Catholic church, there is no resigning. I knew Wignesan to be a vegetarian, but I had no compunctions about bringing him here and steering him towards the aïoli and the grilled peppers, while I had a *salade de tomates*. This is a simple dish which Waverley Root used to choose as a means of testing a restaurant. If the waiter raised his eyes in haughty disdain and brought an unadorned dish of sliced tomatoes, the establishment failed. L'Ecurie passed easily with a generous plate of ripe fruity slices discreetly dressed and herbed.

Being a tolerant man and possessed of a long-suffering wisdom, my companion watched without impatience as I gobbled down a grilled skewer of lamb, peppers and onions. Our reminiscences of Eric took us late into the night. By the time we left I was almost rooted to my now-familiar spot. Perhaps I shall leave provision in my will that I am to be embalmed and, like the corpse of Jeremy Bentham, seated in a glass cage from which I may preside over this venerable institution for all eternity.

It was several days before I would return. By then Mary had joined me in Paris and (with strong encouragement) had chosen L'Ecurie for our one dinner in Paris on our own. I suggested that she join me in an *entrecôte*, which she usually rejects in restaurants because she dislikes rare meat. Confident that the chef would oblige, I told her to order it well done. She was rewarded with a bloodless steak which was still juicy, tasty and tender—the first, she affirmed, that she had really enjoyed other than at home.

Towards the end of our meal James appeared after a long day's work at IRCAM and occupied an adjacent table. He has since told me that he returned so often that he was virtually adopted into the family. Thus, centaur-like, he is now an *écurie* in his own right. I hope it doesn't exhaust his creative powers.

Le Berthoud, 1, rue Valette (5th), Paris ☎ 01 43 54 38 81

There are two forms of eccentricity which would appear to keep a Paris restaurant out of the hallowed pages of Michelin and Gault Millau: a high-profile woman chef and a heavy emphasis on the organic, additive-free origins of its ingredients. One smacks of matriarchy, the other of crankiness. Le Berthoud is guilty on both counts. It has been serving excellent, even distinguished food since the early 1960s, but you will search the two major guides in vain for a *toque* or a *macaron*.

Its owner and chef, Suzanne Knych, does not hide her candle under a bushel. Her restaurant, a shrine to her multitudinous talents, is decorated with her own overpowering paintings. Nothing pre-processed is allowed there; I wondered if she had woven the lace and laid the tiles. Perhaps, with a name so close to *knish*, she grew up having to assert herself. I hope she was not cursed with too many schoolmates who spoke Yiddish.

In the kitchen, she follows a practice which not every famous *restaurateur* would be prepared to discuss. The menu—also her own design—guarantees that no additives, commercial concentrates or stock "starters" are used. This is a guilty secret that many big names have been concealing for years. Two decades ago John and Karen Hess, in *The Taste of America*, were railing against the serving of microwave-thawed frozen packets on bone china at exorbitant prices. Back in the pre-freezer days of World War Two Gertrude Stein wrote of a French soldier who was ordered by his commanding officer to make a risotto:

> *I cannot, my captain, said the soldier, who was a cook in one of the big restaurants in Paris, because I have not the foundation for a sauce. . . .[I]n Paris we always have a foundation for a sauce and we put that in and then mix the sauce. Yes said Captain d'Aiguy and it tastes like it. Let me teach you French cooking.*

Even egocentricity cannot forever hide excellence. In 1989 Madame Knych was made *commandeur des cordon bleus de France*, a sexually segregated honor which France accords its most distinguished women chefs. Wijden commented in 1991:

Madame Knych proudly wears the insignia of her rank on her white cook's uniform while she moves from table to table, ensuring that everything has been to each client's satisfaction.

A prudent hoarder of words as well as money, Gustafson wrote four years later in *Cheap Eats*:

Mme. Knych proudly wears the insignia of her rank on her white chef's coat while she goes from table to table, checking to see that everything is right for each of her guests.

But one mustn't be ungenerous. Without cribbing, the entire gourmet food industry would bite the dust. In his introduction to *Barrack Room Ballads* Kipling wrote succinctly,

When Homer smote his bloomin' lyre
  He had heard much on land and sea,
And what he thought he might require
  He went an' took, the same as me.

Going on a Friday night, I followed advice and took the precaution of reserving a table. When I arrived at eight, I found only one other table occupied. This would be the extent of the clientele until just before I left two hours later, when a young Japanese couple with a baby wandered in off the street, obviously by chance. There weren't many tables for Madame to circulate among that night. In fact, I saw nothing of her until later in the evening when a formidably distinguished matron in a severely elegant suit swept from the kitchen and out the front door. The front-of-house had been entrusted to a chubby young waitress in a dangerously short mini skirt. Within her ample bosom beat a heart of gold; her advice was unequivocal and reliable. Her bubbling enthusiasm suggested that when she was hired, her uniform may have fitted her more generously.

Madame Knych tends to call her recipes by names which might more appropriately be given to poodles: her mixture of vegetables in a cheese sauce is a *Vivaldi*, and her list of desserts includes *cuisse de mademoiselle* (the mind boggles) and *nounour polaire* (cold comfort indeed). Everything suggested that her recipes should be photographed rather than eaten.

I needn't have worried. In the mood for a simple green salad after a plethora of *richesses Parisiennes*, I ordered one as a starter. There arrived a generous bowl of various lettuces of exemplary crispness, dressed with a discreet coating of fruity olive oil and a suggestion of lemon juice. The leaves had individual flavors and none were masked. Anyone would have served it with pride, even in California.

Madame K. is noted for her *pot-au-feu*, another dish requiring restraint. Having been raised on New England boiled dinners, I decided to chance it. Hers came on a large platter bearing a generous cut of succulent beef, a juicy marrow bone (where in Britain would they dare to serve it?), potatoes, carrots, leeks and celery. Each had been added at exactly the right moment, so that they were soft but not mushy and partook of each other's flavors without loosing their own: a perfectly integrated society of foodstuffs. It was a simple unpretentious meal which would have satisfied President Grover Cleveland who, growing tired of the grandiose Frenchiosity of the White House menus, once sniffed corned beef and cabbage being cooked in the servants quarters and ordered it to be served to him, dubbing it ironically *boeuf corné au cabeau*.

I asked my plump little waitress what I should have for desert and she replied without a moment's hesitation, "*Tarte Tatin*, Monsieur." Another simple classic. Madame K's was made with pears, which were spoon-soft and lightly caramelized, but retaining their rounded shape, as though cooked open side up. They could not have been moved since cooking; nevertheless they came on a base of crisp pastry which had not gone soggy with syrup. What topsy-turvy magic was afoot? The tarte was flanked with two little round scoops, one of vanilla ice cream *maison* (I could have worked my way through a carton) and the other a *crème fraîche* which had been made in the kitchen, thick and slightly sour. It was like eating pears off the trees and cream from the cow.

A *cafetière* of perfectly brewed coffee arrived with a dish of *ganache petits fours*, rich little dollops of chocolate cream. The evening had been full of surprises. The showy egotism of the packaging had been stripped away to reveal simple, perfect food which might have come without apology from a distinguished California kitchen. I sipped my coffee and reflected on the sound advice of Mirabel Osler: never judge a French restaurant *a priori* by its *decor*.

Le Hangar, 12, impasse Berthaud (3rd), Paris ☎ 01 42 74 55 44
Trumilou, 84, quai de l'Hôtel-de-Ville (4th), Paris ☎ 01 42 77 63 98

The Beaubourg is so overrun with hordes of the deliberately stateless that its feeding troughs have merged into gastronomic anonymity. Working there every summer at IRCAM (that subterranean Nibelheim where the crude ore of random noise is refined and forged into the heavy metal of electroacoustic music), come lunch-time we of Electric Phoenix longed for a simple restaurant hidden away in a cul-de-sac, far from the gnashing of omnivorous teeth. It would be light and sunny with a simple but not austere decor, the food would be imaginative but unpretentious, vegetarians would be inventively catered for, the house white would be cold and crisp, the tables would be amply spaced, the chairs comfortable, the staff friendly but discreet.

Our search finally reached an impasse: in fact, the *impasse Berthaud*, at the end of which was the treasure for which we'd been searching, the *pot-au-feu* at the end of the rainbow. It was tucked away around a corner where traffic noise and fumes hardly penetrated, so that dining on their covered terrace would not require ear protectors and gas masks. A sign in the window announcing that credit cards were not accepted was an indication that it would not be crowded with tourists. Inside, the white walls and gentle pastel colors were relaxing.

Best of all was the menu, which offered a French/Italian/Californian-type selection of *nouvelle cuisine*, but without the usual Kandinsky presentation and Van Gogh prices. Outstanding dishes have included a cold creamy avocado soup which I had again the next day, a buffalo mozzarella and tomato salad with basil, fresh *ravioles de Romans* with *crème d'aubergines*, an almond *blanc mange* which gave the lie to its proverbial blandness, and a sensational ewe's milk ice cream with a thick elderberry *coulis*. My personal favorite is their *steak tartare*, which is made from very tender and delicate beef whose flavor is not obliterated by aggressive seasoning.

The last time we were there for lunch, a row of tables along one side, maybe a couple of dozen places, was occupied by a wedding party. We were in an alcove adjacent to one end, where two ancient *beldames* were tucking into a Gargantuan feast. They were, a member of the party told us, out on the town for the day from an old folks' home. They were taken away early, having eaten enough to gag a horse. A younger member of the family was a lad in TV newsreader's costume; i.e., respectable shirt and jacket over ragged, faded blue jeans. Babies cooed happily in high chairs, sharing their own little *menu degustation* of the family feast. How did all those French teenagers ever grow up to eat Big Macs?

I would later discover that Le Hangar had been discovered by Sandra Gustafson and written up in *Cheap Eats in Paris*. She gets around. She also knows Trumilou, an ancient and simple bar/restaurant on the river behind the Hotel de Ville. This recommendation passed to me from Walter Trampler by way of Simon Bainbridge; musicians, who are often stuck in foreign cities for days at a time, can be diligent seekers-out of gastronomic intelligence.

The last time I saw Paris (a good name for a book) I guided Electric Phoenix there for our first night's dinner. It was easy walking distance from our hotel and well away from the expensive food factory/showrooms which line the boulevards. Two large dining rooms with old-fashioned white linen tablecloths flank the bar, where academics and laborers sip their coffee or play the pinball machine. The waiters have been there as long as the furniture, and so have the menus, which offer *plats du jour* on a weekly rota, including stuffed cabbage, *blanquette de veau*, *potée*, and catfish with a garlicky *aïoli* which could make you *persona non grata* for the rest of your Paris sojourn. On this occasion I went for their *tripe à la mode de caen*, a tasty dish which is now almost impossible to make in England because it has been declared illegal to sell unbleached tripe except for animal consumption. The only place you don't have to bark for it is at the huge Japanese food center in Colindale, North London, where inscrutable Orientals are allowed by default to purchase their curious foodstuffs.

Appendix (not to be removed!)

This is the recipe for lemon duck breasts as transcribed by Shaun Hill in Mirabel Osler's A Spoon with Every Course *and further modified by me to serve two, after having eaten it there on two separate occasions. (If it doesn't work for you, blame me, not Hill.) It's a zingy version of* canard à l'orange, *closer to the latter when done with sour Seville oranges, which was the ur-method. Of course you could do it with ugli fruit and call it* canard au aegle. *I'd call it* ugli duckling.

L'aiguillette de canard au Citron
(Lemon duck breasts)

Serves 2; American measures

salt and pepper
2 duck breasts
2 tsp. sugar
1 fl. oz. wine vinegar (or balsamic if you're trendy)
9 fl. oz. good veal or chicken stock
$\frac{1}{2}$ tsp. arrowroot (if required)
grated zest and juice of 1 lemon
2 tsp. Grand Marnier

Heat a small frying pan, without oil.

At the same time begin to heat a small heavy roasting pan in the oven at 200°C/400°F/Gas Mark 6.

Salt the duck breasts lightly on the skin only.

Brown them skin side down in the hot frying pan. The object is to extract the fat and crisp the skins without drying out the flesh.

As the skins brown, add the sugar. When it starts to caramelize, add the vinegar.

Turn breasts in the sweet/sour mixture, coating them well. Transfer to the hot roasting pan skin side up, uncovered, and cook in the oven for half an hour, then check. Ducks can carry salmonella, so how rare you serve them should be determined by how lucky you think you are.

While the duck is cooking, bring the stock to a boil in a separate pan, then simmer until it starts to thicken. If your stock is thin, mix a half-teaspoon of arrowroot with a little wine, mix in a little hot stock to prevent curdling, then stir the mixture into the reducing stock. The sauce should coat the back of a spoon; bear in mind that you are about to thin it with the final ingredients. Add the Grand Marnier, the lemon juice and most of the zest. Season to taste.

Neatly slice the duck at an angle, fan out the slices, and surround them with the sauce. (If you pour it over the top you've labeled yourself *ancienne cuisine*.) Scatter a few thin slivers of lemon rind.

I found that the result matched well with what I had eaten at the restaurant. Much depends on the (preferably) rich veal stock—it's the determining factor of the sauce's ultimate quality. If you haven't any stock and no one is looking, you can start the sauce with wine and add some of the leftover sweet-and-sour fat from the frying pan. The result is vulgar but scrumptious. Don't quote me.

The books I've traditionally depended on are:

* The *Michelin Motoring Atlas*, both large format, spiral bound for convenience (be careful not to tear out the pages!) and to the same scale in smaller format, hardback, useful for areas such as the north coast of Brittany which fall inconveniently across the page breaks. The latter's index of small towns is also much more complete.

* The red *Michelin* guide, published yearly, for general info, local maps, and decent restaurants and hotels in out-of-the-way places (or 3-*macaron* palaces if someone else is paying).

* The *Logis de France* guide (available from French Tourist Offices) for good hotels within my chosen price category (moderate).

* Alastair Sawday's *Guide to French Bed and Breakfast, 3rd Edition*, Bristol, ASP, 1997. It's never let me down!

* Its French model, *Guide des Maisons d'Hôtes de Charme en France*, Paris, Rivage, pub. yearly. More uniformly up-markct.

* *Hachette Guide to France*, in an old AA English language edition. Encyclopedic but not very detailed.

* The *Blue Guide to France*, London, A&C Black. Useful for detailed history; the older editions, which are split up into regions, contain more information.

* *Gault Millau Guide France*, Los Angeles, Gayot, 1997. Quirky, snooty; more useful than Michelin if you're splurging but are bored by the predictable.

* Arthur Eperon's *The Complete Travellers' France*, London, Pan Books, 1988. Ten years old, but it has led me to some of my favorite little hotels and restaurants.

* Richard Binns' *French Leave Encore*, Leamington Spa, Chiltern House, 1992. Another very personal, eccentric but generally informative guide, which dismisses all 3-star restaurants. There will be no more editions; Binns has written off modern France as hopelessly decadent and depersonalized. Thank God I still have so much to learn.

* *The French Way*, a ten-year-old translation of *La Grande Bible des Hotels et Restaurants de France*. Out of date, but it has led me to some interesting old-fashioned places that the trendy guides have never heard of.

*Mirabel Osler's *A Spoon with Every Course: In Search of the Legendary Food of France,* London, Pavilion, 1996. An in-depth description of a couple of dozen great restaurants, and an extended essay on the French restaurant scene.

Two guidebooks with planned routes for motorists are particularly useful:

* *Walks & Tours in France,* published by the [British] Automobile Association, London. Large, expensive and magnificent!

* *France on Backroads,* London, Bartholomew, 1990. Similar to the above, but in smaller format with less detail and few photos.

There are good specialized food/wine guides, including:

* Patricia Wells' *Food Lover's Guide to France,* London, Methuen, 1987. Local specialties, markets, etc., arranged by region.

* Youell & Kimball's *French Food and Wine,* London, Xanadu, 1985. A very useful pocket book, with a large glossary. I never go to a French restaurant without it.

Two guides by the same authors, Marc and Kim Millou:

* *The Food Lover's Companion to France,* London, Little, Brown, 1996. Similar to Patricia Wells; benefits from being ten years younger.

* *The Wine Roads of France,* London, HarperCollins, 1993. Even if you're not looking for vineyards, this has the interesting feature of listing restaurants which have been recommended by local winemakers. They're often simple, cheap, charming and excellent.

Finally, a glossy series of guidebooks has appeared over the Dorling Kindersley imprint:

* *Eyewitness Travel Guides. France and regions, including thus far Provence, Paris, the Loire.*

They look like CD-ROMs in hard copy, which immediately put me off—they're full of slick photographs, charts, street maps, and cutaway diagrams. But when I sat down with them side by side with my Blue Guide and Hachette, and compared entries for regions and cities I knew well, Eyewitness came up time after time with the most useful and accessible information. Furthermore, the text was serious, even sophisticated. It ended up being the guide that Frank and I first went to, except for historical detail in the old Blue Guides. Friends who have used the Eyewitness guide to Florence and Tuscany report similar experiences.

If I had to limit myself to a single guide, this would be it. To coin a phrase, don't judge a book by its cover.

Envoi (to Eric Mottram)

As I edit the final text of this journal I can hear in the background a video I am copying. It is of a poetry reading in Paris in 1990 by the late Professor Eric Mottram of King's College, London. Dipping into Eric's work can produce the instant enlightenment which opening the Bible at random bestows on the pious. Suddenly I realize that, during a break in the reading, he is discussing the very cultural process I have been writing about. In visiting foreign countries, as in scientific experiment, observation alters phenomena, "even in France," Eric is saying with a rueful chuckle. The very fact of my *pèlerinage* with Frank—eating, drinking, looking—has taken its rural sanctuaries a step further along the road to homogeneity. If I return to St-Martin-de-Londres and find a hamburger joint next door to the Norman chapel, we will have helped to put it there. I offer no excuse other than the intractable human characteristic which, for better or for worse, has most altered the recent history of the planet: an insatiable curiosity.

About the author and illustrator

John Whiting is an international sound designer who moved to London in the mid 1960s as a correspondent for Pacifica Radio, a post to which he had assigned himself while working as a senior staff member at KPFA, its resolutely high-brow FM station in Berkeley. Prior to voluntary exile, he collaborated with Eric Bauersfeld on his legendary radio drama series *Black Mass*, assisted Charles Shere in the production of successive *Third Annual Festival*[s] *of the Avant-Garde*, and recorded the thunks of students' heads as the fuzz dragged them down the steps of Sproul Hall by their heels.

Ever perverse, John followed a B.A. in English Lit from U.C. Berkeley with an M.A. in American Lit from London University. He divides his time between "making funny noises" (as his wife aptly describes his electroacoustic music activities) and writing diatribes on the state of the world for whoever will publish them.

Martin Sandhill has spent much of his professional life playing with hairs: first, on a violin bow at the Royal College of Music; then on the heads of the rich and famous in Mayfair salons and ocean-going vessels; and finally, embedded in sable brushes, with which he pursues his ultimate career as a witty and successful commercial artist and graphic designer.

Martin's passion for classic cars made him the ideal delineator of the 1929 Bentley on the cover, a kissing-cousin of the 1929 boat-tail Lagonda in which John used to tour the California hills. (John and Frank didn't *really* travel in a Bentley, but a VW Transporter would have ruined the cover.)

John and Martin met as fellow-members of the Hampstead Garden Suburb Gourmet Society. Their ultimate collaboration was inevitable.